Working with Anger and Young People

of related interest

Listening to Young People in School, Youth Work and Counselling
Nick Luxmoore
ISBN 1 85302 909 2

Working with Gangs and Young People
A Toolkit for Resolving Group Conflict
Jessie Feinstein and Nia Imani Kuumba
ISBN 1 84310 447 4

Anger Management
**An Anger Management Training Package for Individuals
with Disabilities**
Hrepsime Gulbenkoglu and Nick Hagiliassis, published with Scope (Vic.) Ltd
ISBN 1 84310 436 9

**Drama Workshops for Anger Management and Offending
Behaviour**
James Thompson
ISBN 1 85302 702 2

Communicating with Children and Adolescents
Action for Change
Edited by Anne Bannister and Annie Huntington
ISBN 1 84310 025 8

Adolescence
Assessing and Promoting Resilience in Vulnerable Children 3
Brigid Daniel and Sally Wassell
ISBN 1 84310 019 3

Valuing and Educating Young People
Stern Love the Lyward Way
Jeremy Harvey
Foreword by Tim Brighouse
ISBN 1 84310 056 8

Violence in Children and Adolescents
Edited by Ved Varma
ISBN 1 85302 344 2

A Matter of Security
**The Application of Attachment Theory to Forensic Psychiatry
and Psychotherapy**
Edited by Friedemann Pfäfflin and Gwen Adshead
ISBN 1 84310 177 7

Working with Anger and Young People

Nick Luxmoore

Jessica Kingsley Publishers
London and Philadelphia

First published in 2006
by Jessica Kingsley Publishers
116 Pentonville Road
London N1 9JB, UK
and
400 Market Street, Suite 400
Philadelphia, PA 19106, USA

www.jkp.com

Library of Congress Cataloging in Publication Data
Luxmoore, Nick, 1956-
    Working with anger and young people / Nick Luxmoore.
        p. cm.
    Includes bibliographical references and index.
    ISBN-13: 978-1-84310-466-7 (pbk. : alk. paper)
    ISBN-10: 1-84310-466-0 (pbk. : alk. paper) 1. Anger in adolescence. I. Title.
    BF724.3.A55L89 2006
    155.5'1247--dc22

                                    2006016311

British Library Cataloguing in Publication Data
A CIP catalogue record for this book is available from the British Library

ISBN-13: 978 1 84310 466 7
ISBN-10: 1 84310 466 0

Printed and bound in Great Britain by
Athenaeum Press, Gateshead, Tyne and Wear

For Mum and Dad

Contents

Acknowledgements

I'm grateful to the many professionals and young people I've worked with and learned from over the last six years and to friends and colleagues who have taken the time to comment on earlier versions of these chapters.

Versions of some chapters have previously been published by the Oxford Psychotherapy Society, the East Oxford Schools Inclusion Project, the Oxfordshire Learning Partnership and King Alfred's College, Wantage.

I'm grateful always to Kathy, Frances and Julia.

1

Introduction

Anger is healthy. Anger is passion, resilience, being alive, engaging. Anger is sometimes an ethical response to a situation. It fuels creativity. It gets things done.

Of course, the *way* anger is expressed matters hugely: smashing things up, bullying, hitting and swearing at people are neither healthy nor acceptable ways of expressing anger. But for some young people those become the *only* ways of expressing anger when no one appears to be listening.

Working with edgy, unpredictable young people – working and never having enough time to get everything done – it's easy for professionals to conclude that anger is best suppressed. Otherwise, it gets in the way. It spoils things. 'Anger management' has therefore become a behavioural panacea. Whenever young people are misbehaving, the cry goes up, 'They need anger management!' I am one of the people then invited to administer the pill.

Work called 'anger management' does go on with young people – identifying triggers and coaching appropriate responses – though not half as much as is popularly supposed. The materials I've seen (Faupel, Herrick and Sharp 1998) are no different from basic classroom materials. They contain lots of common sense but they're not magical. Yet I think we so badly want to believe in the myth of anger management as the solution to behaviour problems that we believe this work is happening all around us; that magicians are out there, teaching young people the trick of how to recognise, curb and extinguish their own anger. We hope that someone will track down the nearest available Dumbledore and arrange for him to come and sort out all the young people with whom we're struggling.

'Anger' signifies different things for different people at different times and in different contexts. We say young people are 'angry' when they're shouting, when they're sulking, when they're sarcastic, passionate, insistent, mildly irritated or full of rage. This book will describe lots of 'angry' young people expressing 'anger' in different ways and meaning different things. It's a book about working *with* that anger rather than against it, about *listening* to anger. Because, by clinging to the myth of anger management, the danger is that we don't actually listen to the meaning of young people's anger and continue to regard its very existence as a dangerous fault in an otherwise smoothly-running system.

As a counsellor in schools, I regularly find myself waiting for a young person, the latest monster to have been sent to see me because of 'anger management' problems. I've usually heard all about this monster in staffroom conversations: about the exclusions from school, the impossible behaviour. I get nervous, not knowing whether to expect two heads or one, horns or just a pointed tail. Eventually the monster comes in, smelling of cigarettes but not breathing any fire and actually looking more nervous than I am.

We talk. Briefly we discuss school before getting on to talking about families: about absent fathers and latest partners, half-siblings and step-siblings, promises broken and trust betrayed.

'I'm not surprised you're angry…'

The monster looks puzzled.

'It sounds as if you've got a right to be!'

The monster is quiet, then breathes a sigh of relief and something clearly shifts: the anger has been heard. Now we can get on with thinking about how best to cope with the situation at home and all the feelings it provokes.

In my work with young people and with the professionals who look after them, I listen to a lot of anger. When I can't hear the anger I get worried because something always goes wrong. The façade eventually cracks and the anger comes spilling out. It's important, therefore, to provide as many opportunities as possible for young people's anger to be heard and acknowledged. That doesn't mean agreeing with every angry point of view but it does mean respecting the feeling itself as valid because, when no one's listening, young people have to shout louder and, if *still* no one's listening, they eventually have to provoke some sort of angry incident in order to attract attention.

I do an exercise with groups of young people. We go round with people taking turns to complete the sentence 'One thing that irritates me is…'. If other people share someone else's particular irritation, they click their fingers. The next round begins, 'One thing that annoys me is…', with other people clapping their hands if they share the sentiment. The next round begins, 'One thing that angers me is…', with people stamping their feet if they share the sentiment. The next round begins, 'One thing I hate is…', with people who agree saying 'Yeah!' And the final round begins, 'One thing I wish is…', with people shaking hands if they agree.

The point of the exercise is to voice as much anger as possible, moving from circumspect words like 'irritate' and 'annoy' to direct words like 'anger' and 'hate'. Everyone gets the chance to find out whether or not their particular anger is shared by others. My experience is that by inviting this kind of regular, structured, verbal expression of anger *and not being scared of it,* young people have less need to enact their anger at other people's expense.

There's a fairy tale by Terry Jones (1981) in which little Molly, on her way home one ni ght, is caught in a thunderstorm and forced to shelter in an isolated hut. Unfortunately, there's a monster in there as well who scares Molly with his noise and size and threats. In the end, Molly decides that, as he's probably going to eat her anyway, she might as well stand up to him. So she biffs the monster on the nose whereupon he capitulates, changing colour and shrinking until a frightened rabbit hops out from inside the monster's shell and runs away.

The story is called 'Brave Molly' and there's a sense in which working with young people's anger does require some bravery.

This book describes various kinds of rabbits hiding inside various angry monsters and it describes various ways of dealing with those monsters without having to biff them. But anger *is* often frightening and *does* often require some bravery in facing up to its threats and menaces. Young people need adults to do this. If adults run away from anger (or pass the problem on to someone else), young people can never feel safe because they've been left with a power which is disturbing – the power to intimidate and control adults.

🐰 I remember on several occasions, as a youth worker, being confronted by situations involving anger where I knew that the future of my work with young people hung in the balance. It might have been on the door at a disco when there was no room for anyone else to come in. It might have involved banning someone from the Youth Centre for some dreadful deed or it might have involved any of the unpopular decisions I was sometimes obliged to make. If I was seen to back off, it would have meant that the bullies had won and that the place was no longer safe for other young people. Always I felt scared. I would get no support from other, law-abiding young people who would have gone quiet, watching nearby. I was alone. I had to stay very calm and not flinch. And, even if the dispute lasted for days and weeks, I had to hold my ground.

This isn't about being physically big or small, being male or female, having a loud voice or a quiet voice. It's just about *resolve*, about facing up to the looming presence, the angry threat, the snarling face. I'm not advocating a reckless disregard for personal safety – situations have to be assessed – but sometimes battles do have to be fought. I taught for a year in a prison and remember, at interview, being asked a question I hadn't expected: 'Do you actually believe in prisons?' I spluttered and had to think. Eventually I said that, although I had strong views about how offenders might be supported once they were in prison, I did believe that there were times when a person might need to be locked up, yes. There are basic rules by which people live and these rules will sometimes need to be enforced.

So, although this is a book about ways of working with anger in order to support young people, I'm not implying that angry *behaviour* should be condoned or excused. Anger expressed as violence hurts people. My contention is, rather, that too often we take anger at face value, as simple hostility, subversion or threat. We don't listen to what's behind it. We dismiss and punish it because we get scared or don't entirely understand. There are usually good reasons for young people's 'anger', as I will describe, and anger is often a disguise, a defence against far more elusive, painful feelings.

Although I've worked with young people in many different contexts, I'm aware that a lot of the anecdotes in this book are drawn from my continuing work as a counsellor in schools, where I have the luxury of seeing young people individually and in small groups by appointment. I'm aware that other, hard-pressed professionals might well say, 'Yes but I don't always have time to listen. I'm too busy. It's okay for you – you've got the time!'

I don't think that time is the most important issue. Five good minutes with a young person in private are better than 25 interrupted, distracted minutes with other people banging around nearby. I hope that this book will help with what's possible in those five good minutes.

I also think that sometimes we have our own, more complex reasons for not listening to young people's anger, as I will explore in the next chapter. This book is not only about working with young people's anger but also about professionals noticing and working with the anger *in themselves*.

2

The anger of professionals

It's a cold morning. I'm about to lead a training day called 'Working with Anger'. Professionals from various organisations – all working with young people – will start arriving in half an hour. I make my way across the car park towards the school building where we'll be working and meet a teacher who evidently knows where I'm going. He jokes that if he wasn't so busy he would definitely be coming to the training day because he needs his own anger 'managing'. Further on, I meet another teacher who pretends to swell up like the Incredible Hulk while wishing me luck and another who predicts that the day will probably end in a fight, 'So I hope you're prepared!'

It can feel impossible to listen to young people's anger when no one is listening to our own. After all, who listens to professionals like these – resilient, passionate people, anxious about anger? Who hears the anger of staff as an expression of passion and commitment? Who's interested in its creative potential? Instead, staff anger is usually heard as an expression of inadequacy, inflexibility or as a temporary loss of control.

This isn't necessarily the case. The professionals on my training day have arrived and have settled in by now. They're discussing the nature of their work with young people *and why they do it*, because we've agreed that there are easier and better-paid ways of earning a living. They talk vaguely about liking and caring for young people, but I push them to remember their own teenage years – the adults who were there to support them and the adults who let them down.

Storr (1972) writes about creativity as the resolution of conflict. I suggest to them that we do the jobs we do – not only to pay the rent – but to resolve or at least attend to something within ourselves which still twists and turns – the wound unhealed, the voice unheard, the authority unchallenged, the potential unrealised... I suspect that we have much more personally invested in work with young people than we sometimes admit. And our passion, our determination comes from that.

I ask the group to remember the ways in which anger was expressed in their original families. Some professionals then describe frightening tempers and arguments when they were young while others talk of anger unspoken, disallowed. I ask what their resultant beliefs about anger might have been. Most recall clear messages received in childhood, messages which, with only slight modifications, have survived to this day such as 'Anger is bad. Anger is destructive. Anger upsets people. Anger mustn't be heard.' I ask what they themselves need from other people when they're angry nowadays and they list things like 'To be left alone. Someone to listen. To be believed. Support. A gin and tonic. Someone to see it from my point of view. To be taken seriously. Space.' No one suggests that he or she needs to be sent on an anger management course!

I think it's hard to work with young people and *not* feel angry. Some of this is ethical anger: a passionate response to the injustice of young lives without hope or opportunity. But some of it is anger from the past, an anger which draws us to work with young people in the first place – young people who, day after day, inevitably remind us of our own adolescent selves. I think it's also an anger about the impossibility of the job, about our best efforts never being good enough, about working so hard but *never* being able to do it for all of the young people all of the time and an anger at those spectators who gleefully point this out. Sometimes it's an anger at being surrounded by so much dependence and need when our own needs are so rarely acknowledged and met.

It's also easy to absorb young people's anger without being aware of it. Rothschild (2004) describes the discovery of 'mirror' or 'empathy' neurons during an experiment in Italy. Researchers were feeding raisins to monkeys and, on computer screens, watching neurons fire in the monkeys' brains as the monkeys reached out to take raisins from the researchers. During a lunch break, one researcher was hungry and reached out to take some raisins for himself. As he did so, he glanced at a nearby screen and saw the neurons fire in a *watching* monkey's brain as if that monkey itself had been reaching for a raisin.

The discovery of mirror or empathy neurons may provide a scientific explanation for what we commonly call 'compassion fatigue' or 'vicarious traumatisation'. Put simply, it means that exposure to other people's feelings has a cumulative effect on us. So, when professionals are surrounded by young people's anger, there's a neurological effect on the professionals *as if* they were angry themselves. Professional 'burn-out' may be the effect of trying to contain such strong feelings over a period of time without having any opportunity to express those feelings. It may be that we eventually reach a point beyond which we can take no more because, when our brains are flooded with sensation, they close down. We stop work or we explode.

What often happens before this point, however, is that our feelings seep out in ways we don't necessarily intend. Working with young people, absorbing and empathising with their feelings, professionals find plenty of 'unofficial' ways of expressing anger when there are no 'official' ways. 'Unofficial' anger might some-times be expressed as physical illness: the body finding all sorts of ways of giving somatic expression to psychological distress (Rothschild 2000). And there are plenty of other ways of expressing anger and disaffection without acknowledging any of those feelings directly – by being late, for example; by not doing paperwork, by forgetting things, by saying nothing in meetings, by scapegoating people. Joking can be one particularly good way of being angry without taking responsibility for that anger because, after all, 'It was only a joke!'

Sometimes it's possible to see 'unofficial' anger being passed up and down a school system. A student arrives in the morning, angry because of some altercation at home. That student quickly manages to have an argument with his teacher about being late for the lesson. The teacher, herself angry now, complains to her head of department about not being consulted over a decision. The head of department, feeling criticised, visits the headteacher to complain about having so many part-time staff in the department.

At this point, some headteachers withstand the anger coming at them and are able to keep thinking clearly. But others absorb the anger of their staff and pass it straight on to someone at the local education authority in the form, for example, of a refusal to accept a difficult student coming from another school.

Again, some education officials may be unmoved by this but others may retaliate, punishing the headteacher with a dismissive comment about the headteacher's school. The headteacher, rebuffed and angered, passes the anger back down to the head of department as an offhand comment about that department's classroom wall displays. The head of department, in turn, passes the anger down to the original teacher, remarking that the teacher's class seems unnecessarily noisy, whereupon the teacher, feeling that she can take no more, finds an excuse – any excuse – to punish the original student (and a few of his friends) with a detention. The student storms out of school and heads for home, ready to confront the parent with whom he had the original altercation.

Sometimes this process is played out over weeks. At other times, it all happens in a day.

There's a particularly subtle way in which professionals absorb young people's anger. Projective identification is an unconscious process (Jacobs 1998) whereby one person gets another to feel his feelings *as if they were his own*. An angry school student, for example, unable to express his own anger overtly, will often wind up someone else – sometimes a teacher. That teacher will usually resist, not allowing himself to be affected by such smug, niggling or cynical behaviour. But when that teacher is already keeping the lid on lots of anger himself, he may unconsciously absorb the student's anger and start to enact it on behalf of the student, becoming enraged while the student sits there, feigning utter disbelief, 'What have I done?'

It's hard to understand why young people do this. Why not be straightforwardly disruptive? What's the emotional satisfaction to be gained by provoking someone *else's* anger? One answer may be that the experience of other people being angry is simply familiar (perhaps familial) and therefore safe. It may be as close to an emotional connection as a young person ever gets because to evince words of kindness or affection from any teacher or peer would be too unfamiliar, too emotionally dangerous. Words of anger might be a much safer language with which to attempt a relationship.

At any rate, knowing this but forgetting all about the insidious power of projective identification, I drove off one day to do some work on anger with a staff team I'd never met before.

When I arrived, nobody was ready. They were rushing around, finishing things off, as people often do when they're wary of whatever's about to happen. The team leader found me to say that she would be late for the session. I waited around and was eventually shown to the room where we'd be working which was completely unprepared and far too small. There was no time to find anywhere else so I set about tidying it up but was still struggling to find enough seats as people were coming in. At least two of these people made a point of warning me, in passing, that they were a team who all got on extremely well with each other.

It was time to start. Several people were still missing but we couldn't wait any longer. I introduced the session and explained the simple task I wanted everyone to do. Immediately they needed this clarifying at length before reluctantly getting into pairs, whereupon the team leader arrived. I asked her to wait until we'd finished the exercise but she insisted on joining the pair who looked as though they were probably the two youngest members of staff present. I watched as she sat down and took over their conversation.

After a while, I stopped the conversations and we came back together in a begrudging, lopsided circle. But instead of reporting the highlights of their conversations as I was asking them to do, they asked me questions about specific young people they were working with at the moment and incidents about which I had absolutely no knowledge. I said I didn't know the answers to their questions.

I was losing confidence and feeling angry, as if everything I had to say was utterly predictable and obvious to these people. They already knew everything there was to know. I felt like saying, 'Go ahead and run the session yourselves then, if you're all so perfect!' At this point, the team leader piped up to inform me that the anger of which I'd been speaking simply wasn't an issue for this team. Others nodded agreement.

I looked at my watch. Still an hour to go. I felt like leaving.

Then it dawned on me that they were getting me to feel their feelings. In their difficult work, *they* had probably lost confidence, *they* probably felt angry, *they* probably felt like leaving. While they sat grinning at each other in ostentatious displays of camaraderie, I was the person left feeling what they couldn't allow themselves to feel, probably because of an unspoken belief that it would destroy their organisation.

I decided that my job was to withstand their attacks and help them find ways of acknowledging their anger safely. I abandoned my plan for the session and asked them to help me understand more about what their work was like. Sure enough – with the team leader making no secret of her own feelings – they started to talk about not having control, about the impossibility of the task, about feeling unappreciated, bullied by the system, expected to perform miracles. Through the wonders of projective identification, these were the very things I had been feeling. They'd been winding me up. Successfully.

The atmosphere changed. Aware of their vulnerability, I felt more warmly towards them. I wanted to help and realised that, secretly, they wanted to be helped. When *and only when* they had said all they needed to say, we began to discuss what they could do practically to support each other with the work.

I think they were angry because they cared. I'm sure they all had their reasons for needing to work with young people and I'm sure they absorbed the young people's anger in all sorts of ways. But what they lacked was any opportunity to recognise and express that anger safely to someone who wouldn't be scared of it and who wouldn't judge them because of it. In short, they needed someone who would listen and appreciate that real people, real professionals often feel angry.

I often feel angry in my own work with young people. I feel angry when they seem to be *wilfully* repeating mistakes and angry when they're let down by adults who should be supporting them. I'm angry when I feel unappreciated and I'm inclined to feel angry when I'm tired. But most of all, I feel angry when I'm reminded – as I constantly am – of my own inadequacy: of not being perceptive enough, patient enough, incisive enough. Then I focus my anger on other people who – surprise, surprise – suddenly seem to be remarkably inadequate!

When I'm aware of this happening and, equally, when I'm aware of my *lack* of anger – when the stories I'm hearing sound commonplace and predictable, when I'm aware of my cynicism mounting – I talk to my supervisor. Together, we make sense of things. I'm reminded that I can't be all things to all people but that, nevertheless, I do many things well.

So we discussed the possibility of setting up regular supervision – structured opportunities for these professionals to discuss their work and its effect on them. I suggested that this might include the opportunity to reflect more widely on concerns away from work as well as at work because the two halves of their lives would always have an effect on one another. We talked about the need to discuss not only what they were doing but also the most important part of their work – the quality of the relationships they were making with each other and with the young people in their care.

They told me that these young people were often very angry. They found this difficult and sometimes upsetting, so we agreed to meet again in order to think about what might lie beneath this anger and how, as committed professionals, they might listen and try to understand it in ways that the young people would find helpful.

3

Anger as a defence

...against shame

There's a cartoon I like. One worm is talking to a couple of other worms, valiantly insisting, 'You two can be worms if you want. I'm going to be a hedgehog and, what's more, I'm going to be the world's leading hedgehog!'

I like the optimism. The worm has a self-belief which few young people would share. They would laugh at one of their friends saying, 'Actually, I'm going to sing in a band!' or 'I'm going to work for the United Nations!' or 'I'm going to start my own fashion business!'

'Yeah,' they'd groan, 'of course you are, idiot!'

Lizzie would have joined them in their groaning. She, too, would have been embarrassed by such self-confidence and would have immediately wanted to mock it.

She and I had been meeting regularly since her last outburst at school. I liked her. I liked her frown. As her counsellor, I felt close to her 13-year-old struggles at school and at home. I enjoyed the times when we were able to laugh together at her stubbornness, her perversity. And I felt hurt when she announced, quite out of the blue, a few minutes before the end of our eighth counselling session, that she didn't want to fix another appointment. It seemed that at the very time when we were beginning to trust each other, at the very time when she was letting me nearer, she was going to end the relationship.

I think that shame and the threat of shame pervades the lives of young people like Lizzie: the shame of being exposed as an impostor – a worm and not a hedgehog; someone only pretending to be cool, confident and successful; the awful shame of being revealed as someone without friends or who is different, someone afraid or dependent on others.

Young people are busy constructing a persona, a self which will deal with the world and its conflicting demands. Through trial and error, that self is built up with accumulated language, with a carefully contrived appearance, with growing practical, intellectual and social skills. Its purpose is to protect the owner from hurt and from shame because shame lurks around every adolescent corner – in sexuality, failure, privacy, friendship – and shame is a crippling feeling. When such a fledgling self is under pressure, struggling to cope with whatever its owner anticipates will be a hostile, potentially shaming situation, young people like Lizzie often use anger to protect themselves, to deflect the attack. Anger looks so strong and powerful. Sometimes it scares off the attackers. In school, a teacher's well-meaning injunction 'What's the problem? Tell me what's up! What's the matter?' dares students to expose what lies behind these carefully constructed selves. And often they can't. They work hard to deflect, deny, dismiss any suggestion that there is more to them than meets the eye. They *can't* reply, 'Well, actually, I'm not as confident as I seem and I hate being the centre of attention. I worry about my appearance and I worry about being laughed at.' Instead, the more exasperated and irritated teachers become, the more students – faced with this threat of exposure – retreat into anger or, when that fails to do the job, into sulky silence.

Writing about research with offenders who grew up experiencing physical, emotional and sexual abuse, Fonagy (2004, p.40) finds that amongst all of them, 'The experience of shame is the invariable and it is replaced by intense rage that is apparently generated to restore the vulnerable sense of self.' He describes how, in a shaming situation, faced with what feels – without exaggeration –

like an 'annihilation of self', the brain shuts down, stops thinking and inchoate rage takes over.

I think that a milder version of this process happens in class-rooms, corridors, playgrounds, toilets and changing rooms. Most young people have felt the power of shame and intend never to experience it again. That intention becomes almost a first principle, an instinctive reaction. So when a teacher asks someone to read aloud or publicly tells someone off or criticises someone's lack of effort – perfectly reasonable things in themselves – there is always the possibility that, for one particular student, this sounds like a personal attack, a shameful humiliation. The student panics, the fear of 'annihilation' kicks in and he or she becomes enraged as an instinctive way of coping.

Teachers dread shame as well. They fight against having their imperfect practice exposed to inspectors, parents or colleagues. 'Unbearable shame is generated through the incongruity of having one's humanity negated, exactly when one is legitimately expect-ing to be cherished' (Fonagy 2004, p.41). They try so hard. When they nevertheless feel ashamed of what happens sometimes in their classrooms, they are more inclined to shame the students sitting there. Shaming is a powerful way of managing other people's behaviour. Those students can't win but they can, in turn, set out to shame their teacher by further exposing his or her inadequacies.

Parents, too, fear public exposure: the shame of being judged not good enough or deemed irresponsible. They, too, get their retaliation in first, angrily blaming their children or, if necessary, their children's teachers.

Counselling is a process fraught with shameful possibilities because in counselling the basic assumption is that something pre-viously kept hidden will be revealed: a real self will emerge from behind a false self. Mollon (2002) describes the way a person will sometimes 'murder' a counselling relationship once it begins to feel intimate and important because the need for such an intimacy feels too shameful. I think this is what happened with Lizzie. I think she *was* letting me nearer but, at the moment when she realised what she was doing and how much she needed our relationship, she ended it, for fear that her need would be exposed to me, another man who would be bound to mock her secret self.

Hers was a story of people coming into her life and leaving. The penalty for allowing herself to become fond of anyone was that they would go away and she would be left hating herself for being so stupid as to believe that, this time, they would keep their promises. They never did.

So she stopped herself from becoming attached. In my experience, boys are usually even more ashamed of expressing attachment than girls. Most boys are fiercely protective of their mothers ('I'd kill anyone who did anything to my mum!') but are completely unable to admit their real feelings of affection and tenderness towards her. So they avoid their mothers and attach to other things. Some go out and make elaborate dens in the woods. Others wrap themselves up safely in the arms of a computer.

John had attached himself to the idea of the Army. He regaled me with stories about surviving against impossible odds on night hikes with the Cadets and about his absolute respect for the hard-but-fair sergeants who 'don't even mind us smoking!' He couldn't wait to leave school and join the Army. But I think his real longing was to leave behind childhood with its potential for embarrassment and begin an adult life without, he imagined, the difficulties of mothers, brothers and tender feelings brutalised by an impossible situation at home. His father would hit and swear at his mother, calling her 'bitch' and 'whore'. His father would then go away for weeks on end, leaving John and his mother to look after the two younger boys.

John had come to see me because of his violent outbursts at school. He talked like an adult, engaging me in knowing asides and collusive jokes. I decided that my job was to acknowledge this adult, coping self, this determinedly unattached teenager, while allowing the child in John to speak as well – the child confused, afraid, longing. De Zulueta (quoted in Pfäfflin and Adshead 2004, p.116) argues that 'violence is attachment gone wrong'. I think that anger and violence can sometimes be attachment unexpressed. John was attached to his mother and loved her. His shame was that his father's behaviour had propelled him into the role of substitute father and, by extension, substitute husband. His attachment to his mother had, therefore, become a love that dared not speak its name for fear of the implications. Fonagy (2004, p.40) writes that, amongst offenders, violence is generated '*only* when it is perpetrated in the context of a relationship with a quality of intimacy'. John's relationship with his mother had become *implicitly* intimate and therefore dangerous. He described her asking his advice about how to manage the two boys and wanting him to be at home with her more so that she wasn't on her own.

I would never have dreamed of suggesting to John the old Freudian notion that boys secretly want to kill off their fathers and marry their mothers. He would probably have hit me! So we talked instead about what was 'all right' about having this relationship with his mother and what was 'a real pain in the arse'. Acknowledging his mixed feelings and acknowledging that they were, indeed, mixed seemed to release him from the pressure of having to be one thing or the other – a child or an adult. He was both a child *and* an adult. Thereafter, his fear of his own affection lessened. His Army stories became less grandiose, less macho. At my suggestion, he started talking about 'parts' of himself – the part that felt angry, the part that felt shy, the part that felt good, the part that felt embarrassed. He relaxed.

In the meantime, Lizzie and I had been circling each other for months after the abrupt end to our meetings. From time to time, we passed each other in the corridor or caught sight of each other in the distance. I could do no more than smile and say hello as respectfully as possible. If she was on her own, she would return my hello, but no more.

We never met formally again. She muddled through the next two years of school until it was time to leave. On her last day, I was chatting with a group of students who were excited and scared about leaving.

She sidled up to us. 'He used to be my counsellor,' she told them. 'Didn't you?!'

I nodded.

'We used to talk about all sorts of stuff. I remember that! You take care, okay?'

I said I would.

She looked at me thoughtfully, 'Yeah…!' and moved off.

…against feeling small

Matthew has a lot to think about. His mum is pregnant by her new boyfriend and his dad has long since lost touch with the family. Matthew is the eldest of three but, for a 14-year-old boy, *he is physically small*. Not that he mentions this. Instead we talk about his anger, his frustration, how much people annoy him. We talk about big feelings, big events – fights, football, getting drunk and being chased by the police.

I think boys who are small suffer a particular humiliation. Wherever they look, men are characterised by size. Erections are, invariably, 'massive'. Attractive men are tall, dark and handsome. Successful men have 'high-up' jobs, big cars and large bank accounts. They've risen to the heights.

Boys who are small for their age don't talk about it. They don't discuss the fear of always being smaller or the frustration of not being able to do anything about it. They don't mention the suggestive taunts of older boys or their own apparent invisibility in the eyes of girls, most of whom would never dream of going out with someone smaller than themselves.

Small boys make up for it in other ways. I work with one who is always in trouble ('big trouble'), who tries to convince me with grandiose tales of sexual and criminal prowess. I work with another who has become a 'huge' problem at school. Smaller boys often express anxiety about their predicament through behaviour which, at the very least, gets them noticed.

Rarely do I talk explicitly with them about being small. It's just too raw a subject. But I do try to talk about *feeling small* because that is what we all have in common and that is really the underlying issue: the belief that if only we felt big, felt strong, felt powerful, life would be bearable.

Matthew tells me how much he hates his mum's boyfriend. I listen and suggest that it's frustrating when we can't do anything about these things.

He agrees.

'I suppose it would be different if your dad was there, Matthew?'

'It would.'

'Then you wouldn't be on your own...'

'Yeah.'

'And you wouldn't be feeling so powerless...'

'Exactly.'

We continue with me second-guessing Matthew who confirms or corrects the things I'm saying on his behalf. He agrees about resenting his dad. He disagrees about resenting the baby when it's born.

'I think it's really hard, Matthew, when we feel small sometimes and there's nothing we can do about it...'

'Yeah, you're right, it is.'

We say no more. The underlying anxiety is acknowledged and, crucially, shared. Matthew is no longer simply a smaller boy and I am no longer simply a taller man.

...against feeling invisible

One of our most primitive needs is to be recognised. Once someone recognises us, we exist, we belong, we're worth something, we're safe. Young people like Matthew – with no house, car, job or other simplistic achievements to define their existence – have a powerful fear of not being noticed, of invisibility. So one of the most important things professionals can do is simply to *recognise* young people, saying 'Hello' in playgrounds, corridors, queues, streets – wherever young people are gathered – saying 'Hello' and, ideally, remembering names. This may sound entirely obvious but it's surprising how often professionals hurry past, grim-faced, staring ahead, intent on the next thing to get done. This rubs off. The effect of not acknowledging young people is to increase their anxiety, their incipient fear of invisibility, 'No one knew who I was!' Their anger can be a way of saying, 'I exist! I matter! I'm here! Notice me!'

Some young people turn away, however. They avoid eye-contact. Their apparent desire is to remain invisible. I'm not advocating some sort of public exposure or sarcastic 'outing' of shy young people but, in my experience, the daily drip-feed of *gentle* recognition makes a difference, challenging a young person's accumulated sense of invisibility and worthlessness.

There's another kind of recognition which is equally important, where being recognised means being understood. Psychotherapists sometimes pretend that therapy is immensely arcane and esoteric, well beyond the grasp of mere mortals. But the most important therapeutic intention is simply to understand another human being. This may well involve training because human beings are sometimes afraid of being understood and throw up smokescreens, 'If you knew what I'm really like…!' But the relief of being understood by someone – at long last – is an end in itself. It changes everything. It takes away shame and isolation. It connects people. When I'm trying to understand young people, I say things like 'Tell me more so that I'll understand… I'm beginning to understand… Hang on, I don't completely understand…'. I ask questions. I test hypotheses. I get things wrong and try again. *Really* understanding another person may require imagination, empathy and thought – it may be harder than it seems – but it's not magical:

'I understand.'

'No, you don't!'

'Okay, tell me more. Help me to understand.'

As long as professionals set out genuinely to understand, psychological doors open. Once young people feel recognised and understood, they're more likely to recognise and take account of other people.

...against hurt

Gemma holds on tightly to her anger, eyeing me suspiciously as I go through routine explanations about who I am, who I'm not and how I might be able to help her. She looks bewildered and fierce. Everything I say seems to be met with an unspoken 'Yeah, so?' but when eventually she starts to talk, she wastes no time telling me how unfair it is that she had to leave her last school because of a fight and how much she doesn't want to be at this new school. She tells me about living with her father and horrible step-mother and about hating, really *hating* her mother.

I learn that she holds on tightly to her anger because, underneath it, she's hurt. But she can't cry. I notice that, from time to time, she dabs at the corner of her eye where a tear might be, expecting something to be there. It isn't. Like many overtly angry girls, expected by their peers to perform continual tricks of disobedience, she struggles to reconcile the tomboy her friends applaud with the 15-year-old girl hiding away inside. The tomboy is so easy – Gemma can strike I-don't-care! poses all day long, sabotaging attempts to help her and positioning herself as the outsider in every situation. In that sense, her anger has become a comfort, scaring people away and absolving her of responsibility. Anger makes everything simpler. She holds onto it and feels safe.

But she's unhappy. As she gradually admits, feeling angry is only part of it. The things her mother has said to her over the years have been really hurtful. It's easy to counter, 'I never wanted you, Gemma!' with 'Well, I never wanted you either, Mum!' but it hurts inside to feel that she's lost her mum and can't get her back. It hurts when laughing boys treat her as if she's one of them and it hurts when her father takes no notice of her: 'I reckon I only get in trouble with the police to get attention from my dad!'

So, instead of taking her anger at face value, we talk about sadness and hurt. We talk about the girl no one meets, who would sometimes like to 'dress feminine' and put on make-up. I have a difficult role because, in being pleased to see her whenever we meet, in approving of her new earrings and in mentioning that her hair looks nice, I have to give her back the *possibility* of being appreciated by a father figure without avoiding the hurtful reality of her own father's inability to notice his daughter growing up. I have to be clear that I'm not taking his place but only, as her therapist, giving her more options about how she can think of herself. She doesn't always have to be a tomboy.

We meet regularly, reviewing the ups and downs of her life. I listen and listen. And then one day she starts to cry and her crying doesn't stop. She *hates* school. She *really* hates it. The teachers don't listen. They don't care. Nobody does anything to help.

By implication, I am one of the people not making everything all right. I don't retaliate. I know the school and know that, although it has its failings like any school, her description is exaggerated. Her feelings about it are informed by feelings about other, far more important people in her life who were supposed to listen to her and care for her and help her. Like many children of separated parents, Gemma has had to take premature responsibility for herself and her feelings. She has had to develop a way of coping and her way of coping has been to develop her anger as a defence, as a way of protecting those feelings which might otherwise have been trampled on. I-don't-care! has now become a wonderfully regressive act, a throwback to the behaviour of a more carefree nine-year-old, testing the boundaries before her parents separated.

So, for the time being, I take responsibility. I offer to write something in her name which describes how she's feeling; something she can show to other people if she wants; something that will help them to understand. I do this sometimes for young people whose emotional voice has got stuck. Then together we look at what I've written, amending and correcting it until it accurately expresses what that young person has been struggling to say. Whether Gemma then shows this to anyone is her own choice. But the process works as a mirroring, allowing her to see herself reflected on paper. Winnicott (1971) writes about a baby's experience of seeing and hearing itself reflected in its mother's face and voice. In this way, the baby gradually learns to shape its sounds into language – learning what happy or sad look and sound like, for example – as its mother instinctively copies and adds to whatever the baby expresses. Through this mirroring or 'confirming' (Klein 1987) process, we learn to regulate our emotions by seeing them copied. Gerhardt (2004) describes how the lack of such an attentive, attuned parental presence affects the development of our ability subsequently to regulate our feelings and behaviour, resulting in inappropriate outbursts of feelings like anger as we grow older.

I have no idea what Gemma's first experiences with her mother were like but I know that her ability now to describe a range of feelings and her ability to tolerate mixed feelings is limited. Hers tend to be all-or-nothing feelings, without gradations. So I write this in her name:

> I am writing this so that you'll understand about how I'm feeling.
>
> I came to Thistle School after I was excluded from Maybank. I didn't want to come because all my friends go to Maybank. But I had to.
>
> It's quite hard for me to get used to new things because I've already had a lot of changes in my life. My mum left when I was nine. Until then, I was the youngest in my family. Then my mum had a baby with another man. She has a new boyfriend now. I still see her but our relationship is bad. I don't feel like she really wants me.
>
> After my mum left, my dad got together with a woman who is now my step-mum. She already has children. I live with my dad and step-mum. I love my dad and know that he loves me but that doesn't stop me and him and my step-mum from having massive rows.
>
> My friends are really important to me. I've got friends in my old school who are brilliant and some people there who don't like me.

People think I'm feisty and hard and I can be. But they don't see what I'm feeling inside. A lot of the time I feel really lonely and empty – like I don't matter.

Although I've tried to settle in, I hate Thistle School. It was so hard when I started. People expect too much of me. School is yet another difficult thing I'm expected to do and, at the moment, it feels impossible. When I think about school, all the feelings I've ever felt in my life start coming up. I feel like no one listens. I feel like no one cares. Everything feels unfair. I wish I was back at Maybank. I wish everything wasn't so difficult. I wish I didn't feel so angry and so sad all the time.

Whoever you are – if I've let you read this – I hope you understand. You may not be able to do anything to help but at least you'll know what it feels like for me.

I write Gemma's name and the date at the bottom of the page, give it to her to read and ask what she thinks.

'Yeah. All right, I suppose.'

'Any changes we should make?'

'Yeah, I don't want that stuff about my family. I don't want people knowing that.'

'Anything else?'

'Not really. It's okay.'

I read the new version aloud to her and her eyes brim with tears. The fact that we've just made changes to conceal some of the information about her doesn't matter: the important thing is that she has seen and heard a story of her life reflected back to her. The fact that Gemma is currently anti-school doesn't matter either. She expresses hostility and resentment because she *can*, because the school will not retaliate and because she knows I won't stop meeting with her just because she feels angry. For her, this is a new experience, a new story about anger being heard and respected, not destroying things and not driving anyone away. In the weeks to come, we'll go on to think about her mother. We'll almost certainly end up with a more complex and useful story than just 'I never wanted you, Gemma!' and 'I never wanted you either, Mum!'

...against rejected love

Young people use the word a lot: 'I *hate* school! I *hate* it when that happens! I *hate* my dad! I *hate* my life!' It's as vehement and powerful a word as they can use. They can only improve on it by adding lots of swear words. And not only is the word powerful, but it offends. Occasionally, I've been asked not to use it by professionals on training courses. Clearly, it upsets and makes some people nervous, perhaps because, lurking somewhere, we all have the potential to hate. Melanie Klein (1935) describes our hatred of the id – that inchoate, primitive part of our unconscious over which we would lose control but for the restraining influence of the sensible ego. The id is dark and dangerous. Klein (quoted in Mitchell 1991, p.125) writes: 'It is the ego's unconscious knowledge that the hate is also there, as well as the love, and that it may at any time get the upper hand.'

For young people, hatred exists and has to be acknowledged or its power persists. They may over-use the word and may use it to cover a multitude of possibilities but, when used precisely, the feeling it describes is neither exaggerated nor untrue. Hatred is the humiliation we feel when our love appears to be rejected: when we reach out and no one is there, when we call out and no one answers, when we love and our love is not reciprocated, when we hope and our hopes are dashed. Describing the earliest love we feel for our mothers, Suttie (1935, p.44) writes: 'Hate, I regard not as a primal independent instinct...but as a development or intensification of separation-anxiety.' It's when the time comes to separate from our mothers ('I *hate* goodbyes!') that we feel the pain of loving her most acutely and are most inclined to hate her for inducing that feeling in us. The same thing happens in later relationships. The purpose of hatred, Suttie argues, 'is not death-seeking or death-dealing, but the preservation of the self...and the restoration of a love relation-ship' (p.44). In work with young people, it's helpful to understand hatred as a *reaction* to the feeling that our love has been rejected and as a *protection* against further hurt. In other words, hatred is defen-sive (Kohut 1971) rather than instinctive. It's safer to hate than to carry on loving and risk the humiliation of feeling that love rejected because, when that happens, young people hate themselves for having loved in the first place. They hate the impulse that leaves them vulnerable and they try to crush that impulse in a variety of ways...

'I *hate* my mum!'

'But you used to get on really well with her...'

'No, I didn't!'

'I *hate* school! I can't wait to leave!'

'What will you miss about it?'

'Nothing!'

In my experience, when young people talk with wide eyes about *hating* someone, what many of them really hate is having such mixed feelings about that person. Only by first acknowledging and listening to the intensity of the hatred is it possible eventually to uncover the love and longing it so passionately protects.

...against loss

Becca sits opposite me, eyes blazing, daring me to speak, waiting for me to say something foolish, something to confirm her current view that all adults are stupid bastards who will never *ever* defeat her. I feel intimidated, uncertain. I'm probably being given a dose of what she often feels herself.

Everything I consider saying does, indeed, sound foolish.

'Tell me a bit about yourself, Becca?'

'Why?'

'Because...'

I could protest well-meaning concern and say something like, 'Because I want to help you', but this will only be met with a shrug of contempt. Why *should* she believe or trust a stranger who says he wants to help?

She throws me a lifeline. 'Why d'you want to know stuff about me?'

'So that I can understand.'

'Understand what?'

'About school…' I'm given the opportunity to try a new opening gambit. 'I want to understand the things you like about school and the things you don't like.'

Predictably, she doesn't like anything about school but now, at least, we're launched into some sort of conversation, even if it is a tirade from Becca about the unfairness, the boringness, the complete and utter pointlessness of school. She tells me a few classroom anecdotes and I listen without passing judgement. In particular, I listen out for key people at school who, in her eyes, have let her down and whom she claims to hate. Later, when I judge that our relationship is strong enough, I'll ask her about her family.

It would be easy to back away from young people like Becca. It would be easy to think, 'Well, if you're going to be like that then I'm not going to waste my time with you!' I could retreat to the safety of a staffroom and lament the foolhardiness of young people today who won't allow themselves to be helped. She would expect this. Her behaviour would have encouraged me. She would have driven away yet another person and been left on her own again. Bowlby (1973) describes the rage of some small children as 'coercive' – designed to make sure that an absent adult returns and never goes away again. The child punishes the adult with anger but, unfortunately, this often has the effect of driving the adult away again. I imagine that Becca's anger began as a response to the loss of important people in her early life and was intended to prevent anyone else from leaving her. But it has become her *only* response, driving people away who know nothing of its origins and leaving her with precisely the experience she is desperate to avoid.

Because young people are *young*, adults sometimes assume that they have yet to experience significant loss in their lives. This isn't so. Young people are well aware of loss and feel it acutely. Their lives begin with the loss of a symbiotic maternal relationship. They grow up, losing other certainties, other simplicities, along the way. They cope with the death of pets and grandparents. Many cope with the separation of their own parents. At the age of 11, they cope with the loss of primary school. Then at about 13 – Becca's age – they struggle to cope with a changing body and a changing relationship with each parent. Some 13-year-old boys plunge themselves into splendid, sullen isolation to escape the embarrassment of continuing intimacy with their mothers, while girls often have their own problems negotiating new relationships with jealous, watchful fathers.

Underneath all this is loss. And loss hurts. Loss is debilitating. Anger protects some young people from the pain of loss and emptiness. I remember Millie, apparently angry with everyone in her life but secretly searching for a new family to replace the one that had fallen to bits. I remember Tom, unable to make friends, hitting other boys all the time, adrift in the new school of his parents' choice without any of his old friends. I remember Jade, whose father had left home, sitting in my room looking unkempt and fierce in best Scandinavian gothic, saying, 'I used to be a pink and fluffy person', and I remember Leon, staying out all weekend to scare his unreliable mother 'so that she'll know what it's like to have someone leave and not know where they've gone'.

Like all these young people, Becca is angry: fighting school, fighting a world that seems not to care one little bit about Rebecca Millington. When finally, tentatively, I ask about her family, she hesitates, deciding whether or not to fight me as well.

She says that her dad left before she can remember and her step-dad died two years ago. Her elder sister lives abroad. At the moment, her mum is drinking. 'What else d'you want to know?'

Young people are stranded between childhood and adulthood. They can't go forward as quickly as they'd like and they can't go back. They work hard to stay in control, trying to hold things together so that nothing more can be snatched away.

Lawson's anger wasn't coercive but was a simple expression of the loss he had experienced. Unlike Becca, he was shy, keeping a low profile in school. He described himself as having been a 'phantom baby' because nobody had known he was there until he was about to be born. His father had lived with his mother, on and off, for the first three years of his life but, since then, Lawson had met his father only twice. He often looked at men going past on the way to school and wondered if one of them could be his father, 'But he wouldn't recognise me!'

His mother had lived with a series of boyfriends, some of whom had taken an interest in her son before moving on. For Lawson, there were big, unspoken questions: 'Who am I? Why am I? How come I was good when I was young but I'm bad now, getting into so much trouble?' His outbursts at school – those times when his anger erupted into swearing and violence – were described by staff as unprovoked and 'quite out of character'. But growing up with so many question marks about himself, he was brittle. Fonagy (2004) describes offenders becoming angry in pressurised situations because they feel as if their whole self is about to be annihilated. For young people with an equally brittle sense of self-worth, a simple reprimand such as 'You've done no work!' can translate instantly into 'You're not worth anything!'. I think Lawson's outbursts were the howls of a 15-year-old boy in pain. He told me about losing his temper in school and, once he'd been told off, once the teachers had gone out of the room, once he was on his own, crying.

It's hard to listen to the pain of a young person's loss without offering sticking-plaster solutions. It's easier to ignore the feelings altogether and concentrate on whatever incident has got the young person into trouble, going over the ins and outs of school protocol for the umpteenth time before asking, perhaps as an afterthought:

'Why do you get angry?'

'Don't know.'

'What are you going to do about it?'

'Don't know.'

Some young people use drugs before and after school to soothe themselves, to regulate their anger. Lawson didn't do this but I think his shyness was a way of achieving the same ends. It cocooned him, making him invisible, keeping his anger hidden. As babies, we see a parental face looking down at us, mirroring our feelings, recognising us (Gerhardt 2004). We learn a repertoire of feelings from watching this face. We learn to express *degrees* of feeling and, as we grow older, we learn about the appropriateness of expressing certain feelings at certain times. But without that initial experience, without what psychotherapists call 'secure attachment' (see Chapter 6), young people struggle to recognise and regulate their own feelings. Teachers end up trying to impose 'regulation' on young people who have never been able to do it for themselves because their early attachment experience was too chaotic: the mirroring face was absent altogether or, in Lawson's case, only intermittently available. Lawson's anger was therefore the anger of a three-year-old, still screaming, still throwing things, still unregulated.

We met for several months, trying to avoid sticking plasters, building up a more flexible sense of a 'father' (see Chapter 8). We tried to understand who the teachers reminded him of as they came and went, taking a brief interest in him before moving on at the end of another school year. We acknowledged that he really *hadn't* had the father he needed or the father he deserved and that to keep looking for such a person would always be disappointing. That father had never existed.

Lawson thought a lot about this. It seemed very important that his loss had been acknowledged. It was real. It *was* unfair. He wasn't making a fuss or being silly. We also acknowledged that our own relationship would end at some point and that we would both have mixed feelings about this which we would need to discuss.

One day he told me about the friends he went around with at weekends, about how they fought sometimes but always stuck up for each other: 'None of them would ever let a mate down!' They sounded like a reconstituted family, offering each other the loyalty they'd probably all missed out on in their original families. He told me about 'free running' with these friends – the excitement of leaping over railings, running across roofs, jumping off walls – and agreed that, yes, it would be great to be Spiderman.

...against feeling ugly

Oliver says of his medication, 'I've got this mental thing.' Tom says of his behaviour at home, 'I'm a little shit.' Too young for a tattoo, Dominic writes H-A-T-E on his knuckles. Curtis wishes his hair wasn't so frizzy so that girls would go out with him. Mark wishes he didn't have spots. Sara and Jenny are both partially deaf but have never told anyone. Jamal will never be as good at schoolwork as his twin.

They all get into trouble for being rude to teachers, caretakers and secretaries. They get very angry indeed with any handsome, happy peers who point out their deficiencies.

Ross hates the way he feels. In his bedroom, he keeps snakes and geckos. His friend Omar keeps scorpions and tarantulas. Dawn, who is 12, looks after a rat and (because she hasn't given up the possibility that she might one day be beautiful) a white, lop-eared rabbit.

...against feeling empty

Sometimes I sit with young people whose stories skip about aimlessly as they recall incidents from the week gone by – snippets of conversation, personal slights and irritations, things that were boring, other people's stupidities – a miscellany of unrelated stories never ceasing until, finally, the young person loses interest and stares out of the window, seemingly unconcerned about whether or not I've even been listening.

Stories like these – half-hearted, half-finished – sound like the dregs of a week being scraped up, tipped into a dustbin and taken out to the pavement with the rest of the rubbish. I sift through, scavenging for scraps – a surprising adjective here, an obvious avoidance there – any link to what I already know of that young person's inner life. Usually I find something that we can use to build a conversation, exploring together the meaning of whatever we've found. But sometimes I find nothing.

'Sounds like a pretty average sort of week, Lauren.'

She nods, still looking out of the window, faraway, thinking about something else.

There are young people who feel empty inside. When they've experienced very little love, little recognition, little sense of really *mattering* as a baby or child, there's an emptiness where those things should be. The feeling never goes away, undermining everything. It makes life feel hollow, pointless. It makes Lauren herself feel pointless, as if she barely exists, skimming over the surface of her life, never able to land, never able to stay in one place. When she stops telling me the details of another inconsequential, disjointed week, there's nothing left for *her* – no sense of satisfaction, curiosity or anticipation – no sense that any of it really mattered. Things happened. People came and went...big deal.

I have an idea. 'What *didn't* happen this week, Lauren?'

'What d'you mean?'

'I mean... Tell me about the things that *could* have happened this week – good things or bad things – things you wish could have happened or things you would have hated to happen.'

'Like what?'

Emptiness is a horrible feeling and young people defend themselves vigorously against it. Food temporarily fills the emptiness for some; sex and pregnancy, perhaps, for others. Drugs sometimes work and there are all sorts of other frantic entertainments which do the job for a while before the lurking feeling returns. Anger is an especially effective way of filling the space – hot rage bubbling inside, people shocked and scared, lots of energy, lots of attention – until that, too, eventually subsides.

And young people use at least three other defences. The first is simply to deny the feeling altogether, so that, in describing a series of recent excitements, a young person might effectively be saying, 'Actually, I'm not empty at all! My life is full of people who like me! Look at all the things I do! Look how busy and successful I am!' A second defence is to project the emptiness onto someone or something else: 'Teachers are useless! This school's crap and you're not helping me at all!' And a third defence is to give up, saying, in effect, 'I'm so empty and hopeless that there's absolutely nothing you can do to help me!'

Because of the empty feeling, there's also a yearning in Lauren which won't go away: a yearning for emotional contact, warmth, recognition; a yearning for the things she hasn't had enough of in her life. It's painful to think about these things, so, in response to my question about what didn't happen this week, she uses all three defences, one after the other. 'What d'you mean, what *didn't* happen? Loads of things happened! I've been telling you! I went on the Internet. I saw those boys. I spoke to my dad on the phone. Me and Michaela went into town and I got a detention for maths.'

'I was just wondering what you would have *liked* to have been doing,' I say. 'It sounds as if your week was a bit disappointing…'

She considers. She doesn't want to acknowledge any disappointment (see Chapter 7) because disappointment and emptiness are closely related. So she reaches for the second defence. 'No, it wasn't disappointing at all! Except with my dad. He's pathetic. If he wasn't so useless it would be all right!'

I hear this partly as Lauren projecting her own feeling of uselessness, of emptiness onto her father. 'How would you like him to be?'

'I don't know,' she says. 'He's just my dad. There's no point in trying to change him.' She uses the third defence. 'I'm stuck with him and that's it! There's no point worrying about it! Nothing's going to change and no one can do anything to make it different!'

Lauren's yearning makes her vulnerable and therefore defensive. If she makes her need obvious by rushing to be friends with people she barely knows, they'll accuse her of being loud, clingy or attention-seeking. And yet if she hides her need, disguising it behind an I-don't-care façade, she'll be taken at face value and ignored. So, despite her yearning, she has to find some middle ground, some way of bearing the emptiness.

In our work together, I make a point of remembering as many details of the previous weeks' stories as possible. These stories do matter because they express her attempts to connect – albeit clumsily – with the world around her. I try to help her bear the empty feeling by naming it sometimes while applauding what I describe to her as her *hunger* for life. I say that her stories demonstrate this hunger: Lauren searching for meaning, searching for relationships, searching for a sense that she actually matters to other people. And rather than warn her endlessly against all that she's likely to encounter as she leaps from one potentially dangerous situation to another (getting drunk, going out with unreliable boys), I tell her that the things she's doing are part of her hunger and that, even when things go wrong, she's learning. In short, she's filling herself with experience which will be valuable. Her defences are not problematic, I say, but understandable, normal. Of *course* she feels like giving up sometimes. Of *course* she feels disappointed and angry sometimes.

4

Anger unexpressed

Some young people seem *only* able to be angry, yet there are plenty of others who can express no anger at all.

> I was angry with my friend:
> I told my wrath, my wrath did end.
> I was angry with my foe:
> I told it not, my wrath did grow.
>
> ('A Poison Tree', William Blake, in Bronowski 1958)

There are reasons why this happens. Alison, for example, could never remember being angry in her life. Her parents had convinced her that good girls, *nice* girls, didn't get angry. Anger would not be ladylike. It would achieve nothing. The wind would change and the angry person would be stuck forever with an angry face. So Alison, smiling nervously, had no language for anger and a residual fear that something very bad would happen if she ever allowed herself to become angry.

Rob no longer knew how to be straightforwardly angry because he had grown up being hit by his father for any expression of dissent.

Marouf could never be angry because his older brother had already monopolised that role in the family. Unconsciously, families tend to allocate roles to individual members and these roles usually balance one another so that an equilibrium is maintained. The role of organiser will balance the role of unreliable family member; the role of tough guy will balance the role of weakling and so on. In most families, roles remain fluid and interchangeable. But in others they become stuck. So, as a counter-balance to his brother's entrenched, angry, shouting role, Marouf found himself stuck in the role of obedient, quiet and hard-working son, expected to do well at school and go on to university. There were advantages – Marouf had the undoubted approval of his parents – but there were also disadvantages because he found himself obliged to agree with them and always take their advice. He told me of his wish to be more like his brother who, away from the family, had an exciting life of danger and girlfriends and extreme haircuts. Marouf told me that he actually disagreed with many of the things his father said but the thought of challenging the status quo in the family was too daunting. So he kept quiet and enjoyed a secret, vicarious existence on the Internet.

Adele couldn't be angry with her mother because her feelings were too mixed – angry with her mother for starting a new relationship but, at the same time, loving her deeply and feeling passionate about her mother's future happiness. For Adele, anger towards her mother was disloyal, ungrateful, unloving and never to be admitted. So we approached it cautiously, at pains always to emphasise that her love and concern for her mother were real and true and were not about to be changed or destroyed. When the time was right, I asked whether, in addition to all her loving feelings towards her mother, there might also sometimes be a *small* feeling of disappointment that her mother had started seeing a new man, or even, occasionally, a *slight* feeling of anger.

My timing was good. She didn't dismiss the suggestion but was able to think about it and acknowledge the possibility. From then onwards, we were able to put together her love and anger as *both* true, *both* real and *both* normal. Adele relaxed.

Whatever their difficulties, I don't think any of these young people had ever stopped feeling angry. They had just lost the ability or confidence to express it. Their anger could only be expressed obliquely. Matty's parents were splitting up. Despite being academically talented and popular, he had completely stopped going to school (see Chapter 6) and lost his enthusiasm for everything. In a sense, not going to school and losing his enthusiasm were just about the angriest things Matty could do, leaving everyone expressing his anger for him as they became more and more frustrated and enraged by his passivity. Our work began by acknowledging the anger he felt about his parents' relationship and, as he found words for this and learnt that his feeling was valid, his need to express it in such a roundabout way diminished. He re-started school.

There are all sorts of oblique ways of expressing anger. One young person might signal his anger by failing to do any course-work. Another might develop particular physical ailments. Another might steal. Another's anger might be hidden by putting on weight, covering a forbidden anger in layers of protection, while others, unable to express their anger overtly, might turn it back on them-selves, cutting or harming themselves in a variety of ways.

I've never worked with a self-harming young person who wasn't also an extremely angry young person. Paula seemed to assume that I would tell her off about her cutting, quickly saying that she didn't know why she did it but that, at the time, it just felt better – feeling the pain and then the relief as the blood trickled out.

I explained that I wouldn't be able to keep her cutting a secret because it was dangerous. I asked to see the cuts because I needed to keep track of whether she would continue cutting now that we had begun to talk. But I also wanted her to know that I wasn't scared. She would see me looking at her cuts and know that, if they did indeed represent something of her anger, I wasn't going to be shocked or frightened of that particular feeling.

I sat forward.

She unwound the bandage beneath a green and white sports wristband.

I asked about the wristband.

It was a Celtic supporters' wristband, she said. Paula and her family supported Celtic.

We talked about Celtic's recent performances.

The cuts were small and scabby. She looked embarrassed and started to wrap the bandage back around her wrist.

'You must have strong feelings, Paula.'

'What d'you mean?'

'I imagine there are lots of things in your life that you feel strongly about…?'

She nodded.

'Where shall we start?'

She shrugged. 'I don't know.'

'Let's start with Celtic.'

'What about them?'

'Your whole family supports them…?'

She nodded.

'Your dad, your mum…? Do you have brothers or sisters?'

Her mother and her sisters did as they were told, she said. Her father ruled the family. Paula was expected to work hard at school, stay in at weekends and choose only friends of whom her father approved. She had been his favourite until about a year ago but now it felt as if nothing she did was ever good enough.

I wondered whether the hurt on her wrist was a physical expression of the hurt inside her. We talked more about her father. I assumed that her anger – currently directed at her wrist rather than at him – would emerge as her confidence grew, remembering things, talking about him, experimenting with conversations she'd never had before, the trapped feelings trickling out gradually.

After she had described one particularly unjust incident, I asked, 'What did you feel like saying to your dad?'

'I felt like…' She stopped herself.

'Like?'

'I felt like…' She stopped herself again. 'I can't say it!'

'Try.'

'I felt like telling him…'

'Like telling him…?'

'To stop!' She breathed out, smiled and started to cry.

When her tears subsided, we carried on talking.

5

Anger exploding

Nathan completely lost it, hurling classroom furniture around and lashing out at the teacher trying to restrain him. For this, he was excluded.

He came back to school the following week and promised that it wouldn't happen again. Sitting with his parents in the head-teacher's office, he said he *did* want to be at school and *did* want to learn. He agreed that, in future, he would ask for help if there were things he didn't understand in lessons.

Three weeks later, it happened again. He swore at a supply teacher, hit a boy in the mouth and stormed out of the classroom, kicking and splitting one of the panels in the classroom door.

The deputy headteacher found him half an hour later behind the sports hall, still upset and claiming not to care. In the deputy head's office he said he'd been wound up by the teacher and by the other boys in the class. The deputy head sent him home with a letter explaining that Nathan was excluded for two weeks while the school decided what to do for the best.

The parents of the boy who'd been hit were telephoned and were satisfied that Nathan's punishment reflected the seriousness of the assault on their son.

At the end of the afternoon, the supply teacher was quite unable to think what might have provoked Nathan. She wondered whether one of the boys on his table might have said something. When questioned, the boys said that Nathan had, in fact, been winding *them* up and that he was always 'losing it' for no reason.

Two days later, the deputy head met with the headteacher and Nathan's head of year to decide whether there was any way Nathan could be allowed back into school.

In every school young people 'lose it' from time to time. Sometimes the incident takes place at break or lunchtime and all the teachers ever know is that the student now sitting in their lesson looks unusually flushed and sullen and clearly doesn't want to talk about what's happened. Life goes on. But when the incident is witnessed by teachers, the school has a difficult decision to make because, however sympathetic teachers may be to 'out-of-character' outbursts, swearing at a teacher or attacking and hitting someone isn't allowed. Nathan was likely to be permanently excluded.

Adults are capable of losing it as well and often much more destructively. But young people are the ones whose futures are damaged if, like Nathan, they end up being excluded from school. Like some adults, they will go on to damage others in later life if they continue to vent strong feelings in uncontrolled and sometimes frightening ways. Because of this, I think it's important to think about the meaning of Nathan's behaviour in order to understand and begin to help.

Young people are fascinated whenever someone loses it. They run to watch the fight or clamour for information about whatever it was that happened. They laugh about it because, when a person loses his or her dignity, everyone else feels slightly superior. They laugh with relief because they're glad it's not them and they laugh with recognition because, if they're honest, they know what it's like. They can lose it just as dramatically as Nathan. He may be the one who ends up being permanently excluded on this occasion but there are others who lose it on the football pitch and get sent off; there are others who lose it at work and are sacked. They flip. They 'go psycho'. At some point, even if they can control themselves perfectly well at school, most young people lose it with their parents – screaming insults, storming out, slamming doors. Some also lose it quite deliberately in more private ways: in the wonderful, uncontrolled moments of orgasm, for example, or in the lurch of secret vomiting.

Whether moments like these are deliberately induced or are the sudden, uncontrolled outbursts which get Nathan into trouble, they are, in effect, moments of abandoned responsibility, which is why young people relish them so. During these cathartic moments they are babies again, abandoning rationality in a brief physical, psychological spasm. Screaming babies are strong, after all. They don't negotiate. Their bodies simply take over. Young people who lose it are effectively screaming, shrieking, shitting, sucking and then, back in the grown-up world, sobbing or embarrassed by what's just happened and trying desperately to cover their tracks.

Nathan comes back to the grown-up world claiming he doesn't care. Behind the sports hall with the deputy head he can't cry or say sorry or admit to feeling afraid so he tries to tough it out. He *is* upset and *is* sorry and, with help, may eventually be able to say so. He doesn't dissociate himself from what happened ('I wasn't even there!') as someone more psychologically disturbed might do. He knows he's done wrong and has hurt the boy he punched yet, in a sense, he *wasn't* really there when it happened. Nathan, the 12-year-old Liverpool fan who likes making dens in people's back yards and watching videos, had fled the scene, leaving behind a baby boy screaming and, for about 20 seconds in the classroom, quite out of control. For those moments, Nathan lost all the responsibility and expectation that goes with being 12 years old, all the feelings filling him until he was bursting, all the accumulated hurts of a 12-year-old life. He lost them all for about 20 brilliant but frightening seconds.

Perhaps losing it provides a kind of psychic relief, a chance to get 'out of it'. Towards the end of his career, Freud (1920) speculates that everything we build up and create ('the life instinct'), we also seek to destroy ('the death instinct'). I wonder how far young people's moments of madness, the times when they lose it, are, in Freud's terms, instinctual: moments when a hard-won poise is suddenly sabotaged by the need to overturn everything. Perhaps

Nathan's 'I don't care!' also refers to those moments in the class-room when, truly, he didn't care.

Yet Nathan managed to lose it in a place with clear rules and taboos which, I suspect, may not have been entirely accidental. What could be more cathartic than breaking all those rules? And what could be safer? Because, in a school, the teachers will always be around to pick up the pieces, however bizarre someone's behaviour may have been. For some young people this may be a much more satisfying place to lose it than at home where the boundaries may never be so clear and where no one may even notice a 12-year-old baby starting to scream. Nathan may have stormed out of the class-room but he stayed on the premises where he could be found by someone who knew him and was prepared to come after him.

In thinking about her patients at Broadmoor, Adshead (2001) points out that, ironically, Broadmoor serves as a maximum security prison for those 'maximally in need of security'. I think schools serve a similar function for some young people, providing the security, the *familiarity*, they need. Young people in trouble at school often settle down if they are lucky enough to be assigned a key worker: someone who will take a special interest in them and offer them the security of knowing that who they are and what they do matters, at least to that one other person. My role as a counsellor with Nathan will be similar. Adshead notes that offenders are only freed to think about what they've done, about the consequences of their violence, about the effects on their families, once they've established a secure therapeutic attachment in prison. Without that secure attachment, it's hard to settle enough to think (see Chapter 6).

Nathan can only think that the other boys were winding him up and they may well have been. Othello is the murderer, the one who eventually loses it, but it's Iago who does the winding up. Iago gets his own feelings *into* Othello who then enacts them. One of the reasons young people are so fascinated when someone else loses it is because that person is often losing it on everyone else's behalf, having been carefully provoked into expressing the feelings which everyone else is hiding (see Chapter 2). Then, once that person gets a reputation for losing it, other people's need for a regular enactment increases. To that extent, Nathan is right: at some level the others probably *were* winding him up.

His may also have been a 'coercive anger' (Bowlby 1973), designed to bring back his normal teacher. First she'd gone away and then her replacement, the supply teacher, wouldn't notice him. Perhaps his was the outburst of a child who discovers its mother has disappeared and runs off searching for her. 'They were annoying me and the teacher took no notice!' All classrooms are psychologically vulnerable when a supply teacher is standing in. When young people are wrestling all the time with attachment issues (Does she care about me? Does she care about me more than the others? Do I dare to care about her?), they are particularly sensitive to a brand-new parent figure appearing before them. Perhaps his teacher's absence was reminding Nathan of his need for her? Perhaps what Nathan then hated was that need in himself and the vulnerable feelings he was left with?

Adshead describes the violence of offenders not only as a way of staying in control but as a defence against the threat of loss. The husband becomes violent when the wife threatens to leave. I'm reminded of another young person, Hayley, who had experienced immense loss in her life and who, as a teenager in school, was frequently losing it. During the first five years of her life, Hayley had lost all the security she might have needed because her father had been violent and her mother alcoholic. She and her younger sister had lived with various sets of foster parents before being returned to their mother who promptly started drinking again. 'I get really angry when people break their promises,' she told me. As a 15-year-old, Hayley went around school unconsciously looking for opportunities to protect others she thought were being mistreated or picked on. Then, whenever the opportunity arose, this intelligent, articulate teenager would lose it in a frenzy of five-year-old hitting and screaming on behalf of someone else.

A recurring figure in the stories of people who have survived abuse is that of the 'rescuer' who wasn't there when he or she was needed or who arrived (as Hayley always tried to do for other people), bringing the abuse to an end. A further way of understanding Nathan's outburst is that, in the absence of anyone else to do it for him, he had to rescue himself from what felt like an intolerable situation. His outburst may have been less of a deliberate attack and more of an unconscious *defence*. However chaotically, he took himself out of the situation. His violence may have been 'self-preservative' (Davies 1997).

Adshead also describes the way an offender's violence can often be preceded by frantic attempts to control *others*. Nathan tells me, when I eventually meet up with him at the deputy head's suggestion, that the reason he lost it in the lesson with the supply teacher was because they were supposed to be fitting some shapes together and the other boys wouldn't move the shapes in the way he was suggesting. He was trying to do it right but they kept mucking everything up. He couldn't control them. I suspect that the 'people' he really couldn't control were his feelings. They were the ones who kept mucking everything up for him.

We sit together, trying to think, trying to talk about how things are.

He fidgets. 'I got £500 for my birthday and I spent it all on McDonald's!'

I say nothing.

'Do you believe me?'

I shake my head.

'I did! Do you believe me?'

Whatever the truth may be, the story he tells is of abundance. In this story, Nathan is enriched and nourished. There is absolutely no loss, no lack. He tells me he might be getting a Harley Davidson. He learnt to ride motorbikes when he was eight, he says. The fish he catches are massive. He drinks crates of lager. He scores goals from the half-way line.

Nathan is physically small for his age but the stories he tells are large (see Chapter 3). I think one of the characteristics of suddenly, violently losing it is that it makes a person feel much bigger. When he can take no more, Dr Bruce Banner metamorphoses into the Incredible Hulk, as Marvel Comics (2000) has it, 'transformed in times of stress into the dark personification of his repressed rage and fury'. The idea of the Hulk has lasted since the first comic strip in 1962 and the first film in 1977. The stories are still being published and boys still play games in which they pretend to be the Incredible Hulk. The Hulk may be scary but there's something very comforting about the fantasy of being able to escape impossible situations by becoming transformed into a huge, roaring, incredibly strong man ('seven feet, one thousand pounds of unfettered fury') rather than being, in Nathan's case, a small, thrashing, 12-year-old boy.

Nathan and I are meeting in his family's living room where everything is immaculate. The indoor plants are polished. Little lights hang over reproduction paintings. Chaos seems to have been entirely banished from the house. Given this, I'm not surprised that Nathan struggles to know what to do when strong feelings well up inside him.

The school has asked him and his parents to come in for a meeting on the morning after his exclusion ends. This suggests that he may not be permanently excluded. Nevertheless, the question is bound to be asked of him and his parents, 'If we give you another chance, Nathan, how can we be absolutely sure this won't ever happen again?'

Schools find anger more difficult to cope with than any other emotion because most schools are full of anger. There's anger in classrooms, anger in the staffroom, anger at parents' evenings (see Chapter 11). In some schools, where staff are fighting to suppress their own anger at the unfairness and impossibility of everything, the first sign of a student being angry is greeted with an immediate prescription for 'anger management training', as though anger could have no place in a school for healthy adolescents.

Young people need opportunities to express dissent, anger, hatred, because those feelings are real and don't go away, however much a school may try to ignore them. Although anger can be destructive, it can also be creative. Out of anger can come the determination and vision to change things for the better. I think the way forward is not to banish anger from schools, but to make space for it to be expressed *safely*, to admit it as a perfectly valid emotion, as an opportunity rather than a threat. Nathan's outbursts are regressive and childlike. They are not a threat to the system. But if Nathan has no means of expressing strong feelings safely, then everything will build up and explode again which will be unfair on those around him and will certainly lead to his permanent exclusion.

Often it's enough for a young person to have the opportunity to sit and, without interruption, tell the story of what's happened: of the anger, the unfairness and all the other feelings. As a counsellor I don't have to do anything fancy. The young person's relief at simply being listened to is obvious, as is their surprise that I should find their anger not only understandable but *positive*. I make the point that what we *do* with our anger is another matter but that having the feeling in the first place is fine.

I remember meeting briefly with a different student, Craig. He said he was losing it whenever teachers shouted and told him what to do. Four years earlier, he said, his father had told him out of the blue that he didn't want to have any more to do with him. Craig glared at me. 'I'd done nothing wrong!' He wanted to kill his dad, he said.

We discussed what he would say if he could kill his dad with *words*. Before the bell went I suggested that, when the teachers seemed unreasonable, they may be reminding him of his dad. He nodded, thinking about that one.

Unlike Nathan and Craig, girls sometimes struggle to acknowledge their anger at all. They sit crying, as they've been taught to do, believing themselves to be feeling sad because to be feeling angry would be somehow unladylike. My job is to give them back a right to their anger and a vocabulary for expressing it because tears won't do a good enough job. We sometimes set up two chairs and move between the crying chair and the angry chair so that the two feelings don't get muddled up.

Boys, on the other hand, have been taught that to be angry is manly so they use 'angry' to cover a multitude of possibilities (see Chapter 3). My job is to help them find ways of describing 'hurt', for example, or 'frightened', or 'empty'. To assume that Nathan lost it because he was merely angry would be simplistic. Anger may have been one of the feelings bubbling inside but there were plenty of others. His outburst was probably the inchoate expression of many different feelings and many different needs.

He talks about his relationship with his dad. He says they used to do things together but since he's been getting into trouble at school his dad doesn't seem interested.

I ask what that feels like.

Nathan says he's getting a new mobile phone.

I ask again what it feels like when his dad doesn't seem interested.

He fidgets, looking down. 'Can we play a game now?' Talking about his dad is difficult, he agrees with me.

We have two favourite games. One is Jenga, where the bricks are carefully piled up until one brick too many brings the whole tower crashing down. The other game is Frustration, where we knock one another off the board, depending on our ruthlessness and the luck of the dice. Both games make Nathan anxious. He risks humiliation, defeat. He comes up against the unfairness of life, his inability to control the dice. We keep stopping the games to anticipate and notice his feelings so that he's prepared for them when they arise and can exercise a greater degree of choice in how he responds. We're practising. We're making his feelings normal, practising talking about them as readily as we might talk about mobile phones or fishing.

Across several sheets of paper, fixed together, we draw a single straight line, representing Nathan's life from when he was born until now. He finds it easier to talk about things happening now, but, as the weeks go by, we discuss and mark on the line key moments in his earlier life: his grandmother's death, starting school, changing teachers, his brother being born, the lizard escaping, the holiday in Cornwall when he nearly drowned. Many of his important experiences involve some sort of loss. Many of them involve feelings which he finds almost impossible to put into words: feelings which I suspect he had no opportunity or encouragement to express at the time. Instead, he learnt to be hard. And the effect of constantly pushing down and punishing those gentler feelings has been to hide everything under a cloak of indifference or anger. Asked how they're feeling, boys will typically reply that they are either 'all right' or 'fucked off'.

One day I bring in a bag of soft toys: dinosaurs, bears and other animals. Because he struggles to talk about them, I invite Nathan to *show* me his family by carefully choosing a toy to represent each person and by placing each one as near to or as far away from the others as their relationship is close or distant. Nathan picks quickly from the pile of toys and makes two lines, facing each other. On one side are the male members of the family, equidistant from one another, and on the other side are the female members.

'Done it!'

Together we go back over the lines, trying to talk a bit about each person and understand how they come to be positioned as they are in relation to each other and in relation to Nathan. He finds it hard to talk about real people and real relationships and his fidgeting increases. Yet this is precisely what he must learn to do if he is to manage difficult situations and difficult feelings more flexibly in future. I can help him understand things but understanding is never enough. I've worked with lots of young people who have developed great insight into their lives and their behaviour. And it can be reassuring for a young person to understand that there are reasons for his or her behaviour and that he or she isn't going mad. But in the heat of the moment those insights don't always translate into *changed* behaviour. This can be perplexing: if someone can understand so well, how come he or she keeps misbehaving?

What makes more of a difference is the *experience of the relationship* between the young person and whoever is helping them. Part of what made a difference for Craig in his rage against a rejecting father was that he was able to tell his story and tell the feelings to a man (me) of a similar age to his father. Initially, he was wary of me as a stranger recommended by a school whose authority he was busy fighting. But experiencing a man who accepted his feelings, wasn't frightened of his hatred, and who evidently liked him however 'fucked off' he may have been, made a difference. It gave Craig an *experience* of being accepted. This wasn't the same experience as Craig might secretly have wished for from his father but it was a parallel one: close enough to the real thing for Craig to take in the possibility that not all men are bastards, not all men despise their angry sons and that angry sons are not bad sons. Someone could have explained all this to Craig but it would have made no difference unless he'd experienced it for himself.

Offering a potentially 'corrective' experience such as this is no guarantee of change, however. I arranged to see yet another student, Jasmin, who was losing it regularly with teachers but who, aside from whatever family experiences may have been provoking her, had actually experienced at least one male teacher making jokes about her in front of other girls. Jasmin hadn't finished taking revenge. Immediately she turned me into another of the bastards and, after one difficult session, never came again, passing me occasionally in the corridor with as much hostility as she could muster from every bit of her body.

Anthony was another young person, also full of vengeance. He'd been innocently walking past a group of boys when something had struck him from behind. He'd lost it, turning and flailing at the nearest boy until he was dragged away with blood all over his shirt.

He was the eldest of three brothers. Their parents had nearly split up a few months before, he said, but they were back together now. He wanted to be a policeman.

We set up one chair to represent Anthony's wild, vengeful voice and another to represent his calm, policeman voice. The voices argued about what had happened in school and about what to do when things were unfair. Anthony switched chairs to speak for both voices. Eventually he stood back to observe the two chairs: his own externalised argument between emotion and reason. He said he thought 'the policeman' had the better arguments, though he could see the point in what 'vengeance' was saying. We were exploring a fundamental dilemma. What had happened to him in school was, no doubt, informed by the experience of his parents separating but we didn't explore that. We simply acknowledged that his 'voices' were real, his dilemma a legitimate one and not a matter of cowardice or bravery.

On the face of it, this resolved nothing but I think the *experience* of telling his story in this way and of having the chance to think about it with someone rather than just on his own meant a lot to Anthony who never lost it in school again.

Meanwhile, meeting with Nathan and his parents, the head-teacher agrees to give Nathan one last chance. It's agreed that if he ever feels he's about to lose it again, he'll go to the school office and ask to sit in a room on his own for a while.

I ask Nathan what he feels about this.

'Okay. Can we play a game now?'

I ask what he felt during the meeting.

'All right.'

I ask what he said.

'Not much.'

I ask what he would *like* to have said. He says he would like to have said about being wound up by the other boys.

Our work is slow. But I'm struck by how much Nathan likes coming to our sessions even though he knows I'll ask him about feelings. He likes the games. He likes looking at the time-line of his life and, increasingly, he likes talking about his week.

I decide to meet with him twice a week. One session will continue to be just me and Nathan together but the other will be a group session.

I've run groups in schools where all the 'angry' boys are herded into my room once a week for a bit of miracle work. They've never had a completely free choice in whether or not to attend this group and they sense (quite rightly) that they've been picked because they're a nuisance. They've also noticed how enthusiastic their teachers are about them attending this group rather than the normal lesson.

Their anxiety is enormous. We quarrel, wind each other up and achieve very little.

So, in working with Nathan, I decide to set up a different kind of group. We discuss it and decide we'll invite a boy Nathan likes called John to join us for the first week. John and his teacher agree. We play Frustration with John and the session goes well. In our session alone, a few days later, Nathan and I talk about how it went. We discuss his feelings about John, about sharing time with John, about how he coped with being knocked off the board and how he coped with John eventually winning the game.

As the weeks go by, we invite others to join our group when we're ready. This is complicated because there are so many sibling rivalries at stake. Nathan is sharing me with other boys and hears me being as pleased to see them as I am to see him. The other boys are experiencing what it's like to be the outsider, the late-comer, the baby in this family. They have their own strong feelings about this and they have feelings about Nathan which we talk about together as often as possible. But an attraction of joining this family is that we do have fun and we do miss a normal lesson, so the incentive to stay and not stomp off is strong.

We put six chairs together in the middle of the room and I explain that this is a lifeboat. It's night time. The boys are adrift on a stormy sea and the lifeboat is very old. Bits of it may be ripped away by the sea.

I turn the lights off. Standing on the chairs, the boys shriek with excitement and anxiety.

In the half-light, I circle the chairs on which they crouch, watching me.

I reach and manoeuvre a chair away. The boy who was on it jumps to another chair and wedges himself on to it.

Now the boys realise that their lifeboat will get smaller still. They joke about whether to push one another off. One or two cling to the centre ground. One boy suggests they organise themselves to help each other but his suggestion is completely ignored.

I pull away another chair. A boy loses his balance and falls into the imaginary water. I tell him to sit at the side of the room and watch. The process continues.

At a certain point we stop. I put the lights back on and declare that those still on what remains of the lifeboat have survived. They cheer themselves, guiltily.

Then we talk about what happened, painstakingly, examining it from each person's point of view and describing the feelings as they arose and as they changed. The importance of this process is that each boy is listened to and his feelings acknowledged because what we've done is to enact something quite brutal, though no more brutal, in my experience, than parts of a typical school day and not so very different from Nathan and the boys around his classroom table arguing over how to arrange their shapes.

They are thoughtful, mostly crestfallen about their part in the lifeboat debacle. Someone eventually asks, 'Can we do it again?'

We do a different exercise. One boy volunteers to stand outside the group. I tell the others to stand, shoulder-to-shoulder in a circle, facing inwards. I tell the boy on the outside of the group to get into the circle, using any means he can.

The circle tightens. The boys hurry to link arms and arrange their legs to prevent this boy getting through.

The boy on the outside sees this. He sighs, takes a breath and throws himself at the circle. He can't get in. The circle redoubles its efforts to keep him out. He throws himself at the circle again and, after much scrambling, manages to get inside.

I tell him to use any means he can to get out.

The circle is even more determined. They fight to keep him inside and I stop the exercise before anyone gets hurt.

Again, we sit and talk through what happened and what people felt at different moments. I ask the boys in the circle what their job was.

'To keep him out!'

I ask who gave them that job.

'You did!'

I ask whether that's true.

They insist it is.

I point out that I only told them to stand shoulder-to-shoulder, facing inwards.

They look confused.

Nathan's face lights up. 'You told us to stand there but we thought we had to keep him out!'

I ask why they might have thought this.

The penny drops for Imran. 'Because that's what you do! You don't think about it, do you?'

I ask him to explain more and he does. The other boys slowly realise what he's saying. One or two look slightly shocked.

Nathan says, 'It's like we always keep people out if we don't like them.'

John points out that they do, however, like Robert (the boy they were keeping out of the circle). I explain a bit more myself and we talk about how they instinctively react to each other in everyday situations.

Nathan is fidgeting. 'Can we do something else?'

We end the discussion with everyone saying one word to describe how he feels about being in the group.

Then we stand in a circle, facing inwards. We put our arms around the shoulders on either side of us, take hold and attempt to sit down on the floor with our legs in the middle but without breaking the circle. The bell sounds. Having succeeded, we attempt to stand up, still without breaking the circle.

Nathan and I continue to meet on our own once a week and continue to talk. We discuss the way things sometimes *are* unfair, like the dice when it refuses to come up with a six; the way good things *don't* always come to those who wait; the way we *don't* always get what we deserve. But just because the dice can be so incredibly unfair doesn't mean we can't have fun with the rest of the group, enjoying the good moments and learning to tolerate the bad.

6

Anger, attendance and attachment

On the face of it, young people skip school because they're angry. They can't do or get interested in the work – 'It's boring!' They skip school because they're not encouraged to attend, because they're being bullied or because they're drawing attention to other difficulties in their lives, including difficulties in their family lives.

Schools work to address all these issues all the time. I want to consider a further, less tangible issue which I think underlies the truancy of some young people: they skip school because of anxieties about attachment.

Attachment theory is simple. It describes the way that we (and many other species) are born immediately and instinctively seeking to attach ourselves to someone who will keep us safe. We can't survive without these attachments. Deprived of them, we become anxious, angry, despairing or depressed. Our development, including the development of our brains (Schore 1994), depends considerably on the security and quality of these first attachments, usually to a mother or mothering figure.

The influence of Bowlby (1969, 1973, 1980), Ainsworth *et al.* (1978) and others' work on attachment theory is all around us. We accept nowadays that the earliest years of life are crucial and that children need to make secure attachments to their parents from the very beginning. We've revised all sorts of childbirth and employment practices to make this possible. We invest public money so that children can have a sure start. We try to help families stay together.

Attachment theory proposes that, as we gradually venture forth into the world from the safety of our first attachments, we cannot help but attach ourselves to new sources of comfort, stimulation and safety. It proposes that the quality of these new attachments will relate directly to the quality of the earlier ones: a child whose earliest attachments were insecure, inconsistent, or worse, will tend to attach elsewhere in much the same manner. But the overwhelming need to attach will remain the same.

Schools are important, transitional attachment figures and most young people find something to attach themselves to in the school to which they are sent. But for some, the nature of that attachment process is more problematic. They are able to make only 'insecure', 'anxious', 'avoidant' or 'resistant' (to use Bowlby's terms) attachments at home and this then affects their ability to attach to school. Their anxiety about making any new attachment never goes away just as the need to make it never goes away.

Given this, I want to explore the meaning of 'school', particularly secondary school, for those young people who struggle to attend (to attach to) it and what a 'school' can do to become a more likely attachment figure and so improve levels of attendance, even when a young person's earlier attachments have been insecure. If attachment is a biological, psychological necessity, how come some young people don't jump at the chance of attaching themselves to something as welcoming and wonderful as 'school'?

It may be that whenever a young person talks about 'school', he or she is also unconsciously talking about 'mother'. This isn't a literal mother ('my mum') but an internalised sense of 'mothering', as adequate or inadequate as the young person's experience of 'mother' has previously been. And, of course, if basic 'mothering' involves attending to a child's physical needs, expressing affection and approval and ensuring that a child feels safe, then 'mothering' is provided by men as well as by women.

Typically, young people say a mixture of things like:

'I hate school… School's great… No one listens to you at school… School does its best… School's always getting on my back… School has no idea what's going on…'

The scale of these sweeping generalisations indicates that feelings about whatever 'school' represents are getting the better of a young person's objective experience. Not many young people can say:

'Well, as far as school goes, Maths is good but I find French difficult and I don't really know whether that's because of me or the subject or the teacher. I'm confident about role-plays but I'm not so good at learning vocabulary. But I suppose that's life!'

Instead they say, 'French is shit! This school sucks!', which might translate as:

'My experience of French is mixed and whenever I feel mixed I feel anxious. Whenever I feel anxious I blame someone for causing that feeling, so I blame my French teacher and merge all teachers together into something I call "school".'

Happily, most young people have understood from an early age that, although she gets angry, their mother isn't going to abandon them and, although they're sometimes spiteful and destructive, she will continue to love them. Most young people can tolerate mixed feelings and anxiety because their early attachment experience was secure. But for some young people it wasn't and they can't.

Behind many of the routine exchanges between students and teachers lies another, unspoken conversation about mothering and attachment. For example, it's the beginning of the school day and Richard's teacher is only doing her job:

| Richard: | What's wrong with these trainers, Miss? I don't see why we have to wear uniform anyway! (*I have mixed feelings about attaching myself to this family.*) |
| Teacher: | Look, Richard, if you're going to be at this school you have to wear the uniform. Same as everyone |

else. (*I want this to be a straightforward transaction, without feelings.*)

Richard: But other people wear trainers and they don't get told off! (*You love other people more than you love me.*)

Teacher: That's not true. We treat everyone the same. (*I have no particular feelings for anyone and I don't expect anyone to have feelings for me.*)

Richard: So how come Scott was wearing trainers the other day and you never told him? (*You love Scott and not me.*)

Teacher: I didn't see Scott wearing trainers and if I had seen him I would have told him. (*I feel nothing for Scott.*)

Richard: You didn't see because you didn't look! (*You love Scott and not me! I hate you!*)

Teacher: [Long-suffering silence.] (*Honestly, I don't love Scott.*)

Richard: I haven't got any other shoes anyway. (*If you won't love me, I'm going to fight you!*)

Teacher: In that case, I'll write a letter home and tomorrow I'll expect to see you in different shoes. (*If you fight with me, you will have to leave this family.*)

Richard: What if I haven't got any? (*That scares me. Don't make me leave!*)

Teacher: That's for you to sort out at home. (*Find somebody else to love you. Not me.*)

Many young people have these conversations, but it's interesting that a conversation like this one so often happens at the beginning of the day because it's the moment of re-entry and re-attachment (I suspect that most teachers' awareness of uniform diminishes as the day goes on). If there wasn't a fight to be had about uniform, there would be a fight about something else. Ambivalent, anxious Richard finds a sure way of expressing that ambivalence, that anxiety. And his teacher shares the ambivalence because, on the one hand, she wants everyone to be part of the family (wearing the same uniform), she wants them all to attach securely, but, on the other hand, she resists the emotional demands of that attachment. Mothering children at home is hard enough; mothering 30 at school feels impossible (see Chapter 11). So, disgruntled, Richard and his teacher take their feelings off to the first lesson of the day, Richard still looking for someone or something, some activity or some group to attach himself to where he can feel cared for and safe.

Young people go to school to learn, but without secure attachments they are incapable of learning: their anxiety becomes too great. The need to attach becomes overpowering. The neurobiologist Alan Schore and others have used positron emission tomography (PET) scans to show how a child's brain develops partly in relation to the attachments it makes. There is reciprocal activity between the brains of the child and its carer (Panksepp, Siviy and Normansell 1985). Schore (1994) writes that the function of attachment is to regulate the affect (the emotional state of the child). In other words, young people unable to regulate their own emotions in school, young people whose behaviour is inappropriate, disruptive or unpleasant, can be understood as young people with insecure attachment experience.

A number of options are open to Richard. When 'school' as a whole feels too unwieldy, too complex, too much of a mixed experience, he can attach to a *part* of it instead. Most students have a favourite place in school to which they retreat whenever there is free, unstructured, potentially anxious time. Some retreat to a particular classroom or department, some to the safety of the library or to the camaraderie of the trees behind the sports hall. Most students have somewhere to go and they find ways of protecting their territory from others. Some retreat to the canteen where an obvious form of 'mothering' is available and is enacted every day. Indeed, the place of food in school is always interesting. Breakfast and homework clubs use food as an important inducement in persuading young people to attend (to attach to) school.

Another option open to Richard, walking angrily away from early morning registration, is to attach to a part of himself. When mothering figures are unwilling, unavailable or unable to offer secure attachment, he can attach instead to his own resilience, for example, or to his stubbornness, his anger, his shyness or some other behaviour. Any of these parts of a person can become powerful allies, clung to desperately and making the world of school feel much safer and simpler. When a teacher unwittingly tries to separate a student from this attached part of himself ('Why are you so angry?') the results can be spectacular.

It's easy for students to be characterised in the staffroom as 'angry' ('He needs anger management!') if that's the only part of a student on display, the part to which he is so clearly and so vehemently attached. Young people get stuck with anger for one good reason: stuckness is safe. If we know that we'll be angry in every human interaction, relationships become wonderfully straightforward, wonderfully safe.

Helping a young person to develop a more flexible set of responses, a broader role repertoire, takes time. Bannister (2002) has written about the beneficial effect of creative therapies with sexually abused children whose attachment experience has been cruelly damaging. She shows how creative play between an abused child and a therapist forms a new attachment where none was possible before. I think the same principle applies in schools with older young people like Richard whose experience has been less traumatic but who are nevertheless finding attachment difficult.

Learning to play and have fun with someone else is an early developmental process and often young people need to be returned to this formative process in order to re-learn the process of attachment. Scores of young people report that they 'just want to have fun', but their way of having fun in school is full of anxiety because it remains unstructured and subversive. They hit one another but they are 'only playing, Miss!' They tease one another but 'only as a joke, Sir!' Whenever teachers and students have opportunities to play together in safe, structured ways (through sport, experiments, drama, art, music, trips and practical subjects, for example) the possibility exists for some young people of making a more secure, lasting attachment to the experience of 'school'.

Despite all their anxieties, the vast majority of young people do attend school, however. I think there's a sense in which they can attach to a collective assumption. There might be the same assumption in cults or gangs: an assumption about the importance of remaining in the group, about the importance of its leader or the importance of its members. Such an assumption can make life feel very secure for the insiders. It may be that more young people don't run away from boarding schools because there's an equally strong collective assumption that 'school' is good or character-building or simply inevitable. I imagine that in some countries an assumption exists that education is intrinsically good, however financially impoverished a school might be. Despite attempts by politicians in prosperous countries to develop a similarly strong collective assumption about the security and prosperity afforded by education, many young people remain unconvinced. Their aspirations are different and an alternative educational experience awaits them at home anyway: an Internet attachment which they can control and which comes in tastier bites than drawn-out lessons in dilapidated, noisy classrooms.

But, in the meantime, Richard, in the wrong kind of shoes, sitting in the same corner of the library every break and lunchtime, eating crisps, monopolising the computer and picking fights with the librarian, has another obvious option. He can skip school altogether.

Away from school, he can look for other attachments. He can retreat to the arms of a possibly collusive parent or stay in bed (a lovely, warm, womb-like attachment). He can spend all day attached to a biddable computer or television. He can find an alternative place to hang out in town and attach himself to the young people he meets there who may share a collective assumption about the *uselessness* of 'school'. I think it's helpful to think of whatever he does when he skips school as – on the level I'm describing – his continuing search for secure attachments. The attachments he manages to make may well be self-destructive (drugs, cars, dodgy friends) but Richard may experience them nevertheless as more secure than the 'school' he is currently avoiding. So, in the face of such powerful needs, how can a school become a more likely attachment figure?

Schools already do lots of sensible things. They make rules and expectations as clear and simple, as consistent and reliable as possible. They think hard about welcoming new cohorts of students and try to ensure that there is always continuity of care. They work mightily on behalf of all students. But I want to highlight some further dynamics which are related to the process of attachment and, therefore, attendance.

Skipping school asks lots of implicit questions such as: 'Am I noticed? Do I matter? What's worth getting out of bed for? How powerful am I? Why is everything imperfect?' Schools sometimes get into difficulties with these big existential questions because so much of school is about knowing the answers. These more fundamental questions which young people are always asking – sometimes inarticulately and sometimes through their behaviour – are frequently dismissed as irrelevant or are answered with bland, defensive certainties. Acknowledging the importance of such questions seems a more productive first step and acknowledging that uncertainty is real seems a more useful way forward than resorting to cheap, superficial answers.

'Why should I go to school?'

'Good question!'

'What's the point?'

'Good question again! Let's think about the point of anything...'

Many teachers get understandably defensive because these questions tap into uncertainties of their own of which they would rather not be reminded. After all, to remain committed to the difficult job of teaching, they must believe that their school is improving; they must believe that there's a purpose. Understandably, they hate the prospect of uncertainty, whereas I think that, for a lot of young people, uncertainty is a philosophical preoccupation that needs to be properly acknowledged. Until such troubling questions are heard, they'll continue to be asked.

Skipping school is also an expression of real disappointment (see Chapter 7). Every year schools are obliged to sell themselves and every year what they offer to prospective students looks better than the year before. The message is that if you join this consistently improving school, the facilities will be excellent, the extra-curricular activities innumerable, lessons will always be exciting and the world will be your oyster. Although their experience so far has taught them that any 'school' is unlikely to live up to its promises, almost every young person gives the new one a try, and yet, although every school's prospectus is more glossy than before, the attendance statistics of some schools remain frustratingly poor.

While I think it's important to be positive and offer hope to young people, I think schools underestimate the effect of the disappointment inflicted on students every year when they find out that the promised computers won't be available after all, the school play will have to be postponed, the teacher they told about the bullying did nothing about it and the teacher who started the Chess Club now comes late or cancels at the last minute. These things happen in schools on an almost daily basis and young people try to be understanding. But what really hurts is the disappointment of so many impulsive promises made only to be broken.

I think it's much better not to make the promise in the first place but to keep the rhetoric realistic. 'We're all working very hard to improve but this school is still imperfect and always will be imperfect, like the rest of the world.' Young people are more likely to attach to something that is what it seems. Rash promises turn 'school' into such a tantalising mothering figure that young people – desperate to attach – will seek to attach all over again, despite all their previous disappointments. But this time, when the disappointment comes, when the tantalising promise is broken or simply forgotten about, it's too much of a reminder for some to bear. They register their feelings in the most powerful way they can – by skipping school altogether. They get as far away from the source of those disappointed feelings as possible.

One of the characteristics of really *effective*, successful truancy is that it gets teachers to feel all the feelings the young person is feeling. Teachers find themselves feeling angry, frustrated, helpless or indifferent. Richard gets his teachers to feel all his own feelings and, the longer he stays away from school, the more acute those feelings become for his teachers. At various stages, they feel angry with him, frustrated by him, unable to help him or simply indifferent towards him.

When young people approach 'school' ambivalently, cautiously, fearing that their previously unsatisfactory experiences of attachment will be repeated, they will always find someone in school unwittingly prepared to repeat the pattern and prove that this 'school' really is no different. So, for example, after weeks of work by professionals behind the scenes, trying to get him back into school, Richard does come back, wearing the right shoes this time, but late. Quite properly, he goes to Reception to register his presence:

Richard:	I'm here. (*I'm feeling more mixed than ever.*)
Receptionist:	Well, what a surprise! We're honoured! Didn't think we'd see you again. Have you got a note? (*Your absence has made us all feel worthless and so I want you to feel some of that.*)
Richard:	No, my mum didn't have time. I'll bring one tomorrow. (*I'm sorry.*)
Receptionist:	Well, make sure you do! Anyway, as you're here now, you'd better get off to your lesson. (*You're worthless, okay?*)
Richard:	Where did you think I'd go? (*No, I'm not!*)
Receptionist:	Don't be rude! (*Yes, you are!*)
Richard	[Swears at the receptionist and walks out of school again.]

Attachment requires a reciprocal relationship. The mothering figure has to be prepared to receive and respond to the attachment and many teachers are understandably alarmed by attachment. In training sessions, when we're considering the underlying needs of students like Richard, I'm always asked, 'What if he becomes too attached? What if he becomes dependent?' From the way professionals talk, it can sound as if dozens of students are out there, all wanting to be suckled and held between lessons. The fantasy is out of proportion to the objective likelihood of even one student behaving like this. But the assumption, the inkling many teachers have that students will want to attach, is absolutely right.

They energetically resist that attachment. The very idea of attachment is denigrated in most secondary school staffrooms. Any teacher perceived as getting 'too close' to a student is thought of as vaguely unprofessional, as giving in to something dangerous. In corridors, intimacy and fondness between boys is seen as especially frightening. Nostalgia is childish. Young people who skip school are not regarded as heroes but are usually scorned by their peers for being somehow weak, childish, cowardly. The institutional defensiveness is as powerful as the need for attachment that it works so hard to resist.

Another experience which I think disappoints young people at the very start of secondary school is hearing whatever attachment they may have felt towards their primary school denigrated: 'This is big school now – you leave behind childish things – I don't know what happened at your last school but in this school we don't tolerate behaviour like that!' The loss of primary school and all that it meant is rarely dwelt upon or respected. It therefore becomes harder for some young people to attach to the big new school when their loyalty to the old one is derided in this sometimes quite brutal way. It's true that young people's behaviour can seem especially childish just before or just after a transition, but this may be more about their anxiety than about any gratuitous silliness. Whenever we take a big jump, we always step backwards. Sometimes the prospect of a new school, a new year group or some other important transition is used by teachers as a threat ('You won't be able to do that when...!'), which only increases the anxious behaviour. Pincus (1976, p.129) writes that 'to tolerate separation anxiety and to mourn are signs of the healthy personality who is capable of deep attachment. Without real attachments, secure autonomy cannot be achieved.' But when the prevailing school culture is about always looking forwards and never looking backwards, I think some young people experience a splitting of themselves into a grown-up part (the future) and a child part (the past): a split they struggle to manage but which would be easier if secondary schools promoted a more sympathetic attitude towards the immediate past.

Part of the problem is that no one offers any 'mothering' to the mothering figures. The teacher trying to deal with Richard's trainers in morning registration keeps him at arm's length partly for fear of being overwhelmed by his underlying needs. Her own needs are not attended to. There's no one for her to talk with about the cumulative effect of managing hundreds of human relationships each week and there's no expectation that a good teacher (which she is) will ever need to talk through the emotional effects of the work and the tangled feelings which inevitably arise (see Chapter 11). Defensive, stressed teachers do not make secure attachment figures.

So, part of the solution would be for a school to acknowledge that such needs do exist for teachers and that, unacknowledged, they eventually get in the way of productive working relationships. It ought then to be possible to set up a system of professional, non-managerial support, thinking through and disentangling relationships, helped by someone employed from outside the institution – a system of which good teachers can take advantage as an inevitable part of their difficult work and as an essential part of professional development. Teachers can more easily remain open to the attachment needs of their students if they have a place to take their own reciprocal needs and concerns. Students can only attach to someone who is available.

Schools understand the importance of getting off to a good start and they plan ahead meticulously. But although they are experts at beginnings, they are usually much less good at endings because, by the time a student or class is ready to move on, the teacher is full of misgivings: glad they are moving on in some ways but, in other ways, sad to see the back of them (Luxmoore 2000). The simplest thing for a teacher to do (in the absence of any help in thinking about it) is to feel neither glad nor sad, but to deal with the situation mechanically, avoiding even mentioning the ending or acknowledging that anyone might have strong (and sometimes strongly mixed) feelings about it. In this way, teachers keep their own feelings of attachment to students shamefully hidden. But when nothing has been properly ended, when part of themselves has been left behind, it's much harder for students to begin again, year after year, and re-attach wholeheartedly to new classrooms, new teachers, new peers.

Some young people, struggling to come to school regularly, say, 'I only come to see my friends!' I remember working with one boy who was almost literally attached to his mobile phone. It contained the numbers of all his friends and he spent large parts of the day speaking to them, reassuring himself that they were still there and were still his friends. Getting excluded from school was upsetting but not half as upsetting as when his parents decided to punish him further by taking away his phone. As an attachment object, it had come to represent who he was and what he was worth. He had even become an expert at dismantling and repairing mobile phones so that his friends were never without one. 'My mobile,' he told me, 'is my life.'

If the security of attachment is, for some young people, to be found in peer relationships, schools can devise ways in which students themselves might further support one another. There are all sorts of models whereby older students can work with and befriend younger ones in a variety of creative ways or whereby students who are recognised as having street credibility can be available to support their peers in times of crisis. All the models

require those students offering the support to be trained and con-
tinually supervised (mothering the mothering figures) but, over
time, an ethos can develop whereby students are free to attach to
more of their peers than they might otherwise do because the prevailing student culture now makes that permissible (Luxmoore
2000).

Another difficulty for young people struggling to attend school
is the sense in which 'school' can come to seem like a rival rather
than additional attachment. Yearning for home, like yearning for
primary school and yearning for the past, is often seen in schools as
dangerously regressive and something to be grown out of as
quickly as possible. The rivalry between schools and parents (and
there is *always* an implicit rivalry) forces some young people to
make an emotional choice because it's hard to sustain an equal
attachment to people who dislike or mistrust one another. Many
schools do make huge efforts to welcome and value the contribution of parents but, in terms of attachment, the rivalry remains a
deep one because teachers *are* parent figures, they *are* potential
attachment figures. I think parents are well aware of this and,
perhaps for those who worry most about their own parenting skills,
it's unsettling. Keeping a son or daughter at home may provide
company for a depressed parent but it's also a good, covert way of
attacking and diminishing the importance of 'school' as a rivalrous
attachment figure. Some schools have been able to employ home–
school link workers who, without the baggage of courts, the police
and officialdom, can intercede and lessen that sense of rivalry.

It's surprising that secondary schools don't make more use of
grandparent figures, given the fact that grandparents are sometimes
much more secure attachment figures for young people than their
embattled or distracted parents. Where grandparent figures are
available in schools (usually in some non-teaching capacity) they
are often regarded with great affection and are often confided in by
certain students for whom their presence makes a real difference.

I've wondered about the effect of teachers visiting their students' homes. In one school I suggested this, wanting to compare

the attendance records of the class whose tutor made an annual home visit with the class whose tutor didn't. I had some extra money to pay the home-visiting tutor. But the idea was instantly dismissed because everyone's workload was already far too great. Without a doubt.

Workload is an absolutely real problem for teachers but I was interested in the school's refusal even to think about what it would be like. I wondered whether the school's reaction was partly about needing to hold on to a collective assumption of its own, to the security of an old rivalry, the sense of parents as an unreliable enemy to be neither trusted nor appeased. I wondered whether a planned home visit (not occasioned by any crisis) might simply lessen the rivalry. Some young people undoubtedly dread the idea of a teacher coming round for a cup of tea because they are so used to the idea that school relationships must be alternative relationships. But I think that there are other young people for whom that sense of school as a rival rather than additional attachment figure involves making a choice. And in skipping school, they indicate the choice they have made.

Anyway, after months away, Richard has agreed to give 'school' yet another try and has persuaded the authorities to let him start at a new one. He's heard really good things about this school and some of his friends go there.

It's his first day. Still desperate for attachment, he wanders nervously towards the gates...

7

Anger and disappointment

Kerry is about to be excluded from school. Again. This time she's told her biology teacher, Miss Roberts, to 'fuck off, you bitch!'

We meet for our counselling session, as we'd arranged to do last week, long before the Miss Roberts incident happened. But once we finish today, Kerry must go straight to the headteacher's office where she will be excluded for four days.

Exclusions make the chances of young people succeeding in school less likely. The headteacher knows this but has no choice because, at this late stage in her school career, Kerry has exhausted all the other options. Excluding her will offer clear support for Miss Roberts, who is in her first year of teaching. It will send a message to other students that swearing at teachers is forbidden and that Miss Roberts, however inexperienced she may be, is to be treated with as much respect as anyone. Exclusion will also make it clear to Kerry, once again, that there are limits.

It's not the first time that Kerry has been excluded. She will have known, as soon as she swore at Miss Roberts in front of the class, that, unless Miss Roberts pretended not to hear, she would end up being excluded.

Miss Roberts, quite rightly, did hear and did react. Miss Roberts had far too much to lose.

'So why did you do it?' the headteacher will ask her. 'When we're getting so close to the exams? You must have known...?'

Kerry will shrug her I-don't-know-and-I-don't-care shoulders and say nothing.

'I hate Miss Roberts! She's a bitch!' she tells me. 'She can't keep control of us. Whenever I put my hand up to ask something she ignores me. But she's always helping the boys!'

I remind Kerry that, only a few months earlier, she identified Miss Roberts as the one teacher she really liked. She stayed behind after lessons and chatted to Miss Roberts, who, at the time, seemed pleased to be confided in and trusted by Kerry.

'We got on all right,' Kerry confirms, 'but that was *before.*'

I wonder to myself what 'before' means. In my experience, many young people have an abiding sense of a world that was meant to be, a world 'before'. It's a lovely world full of fun and friendship, closeness and entirely unconditional love. People are kind. The surroundings are calm and peaceful. It is, perhaps, Freud's (1927) original world of 'oceanic feeling' between ourselves and our environment or Balindt's (1968) world, even before birth, when we are in an 'harmoniously interpenetrating mix-up' with the external world. Meltzer describes an 'aesthetic position' where a new-born baby experiences, however fleetingly, the absolute, intense beauty of its mother (Meltzer and Williams 1988). He suggests that there is a brief period of mutual beatification between mother and baby. This may be what young people allude to when they describe a lovely world, now seemingly lost to them. Even the most hardened young people can describe this world with surprising ease. Coming to terms with the loss of it is one of the things which most upsets, confuses and enrages them. Because that world seemed so lovely, it hurts like hell to be deprived of it.

Its loss is apparent for adults too. I've run psychotherapy groups where members have expressed the rage, grief, hurt and frustration that they've kept locked away unproductively for often hideously long periods of time. But when all that is over and their energy is spent, their need is often for a conciliatory experience, usually with a mother or father. Many have no conscious recollection of such an experience in their lives and yet somehow they can imagine it vividly. Parent and child sit together, the parent typically cradling the child. They are outdoors sometimes, beside a tree, on a hillside or by water. Always the scene is peaceful and simple and still.

I think Kerry's fantasy is of just such a closeness with people like Miss Roberts. Throughout her school life she has searched for them, finding them sometimes in other people's parents and sometimes in teachers. Recently, she found one of them in a boyfriend. For a while he, too, was the most marvellous person who understood her implicitly and to whom she could talk about anything. He was her soul-mate, brother, best friend, someone she couldn't imagine ever being without.

But that was before a different reality set in as it did with all the others including, now, Miss Roberts. These people had other lives as well. They had their own needs and sometimes they had different opinions. They didn't always have time for Kerry.

The disillusionment is too awful to bear. Kerry hates it and, in order to keep herself blameless and pure, turns them into ogres in her mind, trying her best to get them all to hate her. In getting Miss Roberts to report her for swearing, Kerry convinces herself that Miss Roberts never really cared and was never really interested. Like her predecessors, Miss Roberts can now be accused of failing Kerry.

It's easy to conclude that Kerry's struggle is really about accepting the parents she has rather than the ones of whom she dreams. This is partly true. But what's interesting is where her dream comes from and why it persists as a possibility for Kerry and so many other young people for so long, despite all their accumulating experience to the contrary. I remember 24-year-old Suzie, still torturing herself with her boyfriend's inability to be the perfectly benign man she wished him to be. I remember 19-year-old Simon dreaming of meeting up with his father, hoping that his father would be changed from the man who once drove Simon and his mother into refuges before his mother was finally able to let go (perhaps of her own dream) and get a divorce. I remember countless other young people, all wishing that their parents would get back together and be a happy family again. It's hard to let go of such a dream.

Much has been written about adolescence as the re-enactment of infantile experience, as a period of mourning for lost attachments. I think the extent to which young people are able to describe so readily an alternative world they believe was meant to be, even when their life experience since birth has been disastrous, may indicate some unconscious recollection of a life before birth when things really *were* like that, when they were safe and secure in symbiotic relationship with their mothers. Whoever they are, all young people really *did* once have that experience.

Andy is another example. He says he's never read the book and only seen snatches of the film, but when it comes up in our conversation, he seems to understand almost instinctively what *The Secret Garden* (Hodgson Burnett 1911) is all about. His family is similarly broken up. In trying to understand why this happened, we talk about his secret garden and what it must have been like. *Before.*

He pictures it vividly. His mum and dad are there. And his sister. And a friend he had when he was little who moved away. They have picnics together. They play with animals and they plant things. They make tree houses and dens. No one ever comes to disturb them in the garden. And, when the sun goes down, they all fall asleep in a hammock.

I suggest to Andy that he's been keeping this garden secret in his heart. He agrees. By showing me around his garden, he re-connects it with the outside world in a way that I believe is helpful. For, as long as his garden remains secret, locked away inside Andy, no one can understand a most important part of him and, as in the book, the danger is that this emotional garden becomes overgrown and uncared for, more and more cut off from the ordinary realities of other people.

Most work with young people ends up being about learning to adapt to the world around us. Winnicott (1965a) writes about the frightening 'I AM moment' when the child first learns to distinguish itself from its mother. Lacan (1949) describes this same moment as the child's first experience of existential alienation in the world. Freud (1911), too, describes our gradual progression

from an early world of instinctual gratification, 'the pleasure principle', to the more demanding 'reality principle' whereby we learn
that other people are not necessarily within our control, whereby
we must often wait for gratification, whereby there exists a reality
external to our selves. Years later, Winnicott (1975, p.240) writes
that 'the task of reality acceptance is never completed, …[and] no
human being is free from the strain of relating inner and outer
reality'.

Young people wrestle with this process of adaptation. They
remember a lovely and now seemingly lost world and are learning, in
however roundabout a way, to talk about that loss. Kerry is less
adept. When she realises that Miss Roberts is not the fantasy figure
she imagined, 'Fuck off!' becomes her way of talking about that.
And exclusion becomes the school's way of telling Kerry to find a
more sophisticated way of talking about her disappointment.

A week later, she returns from exclusion. Nothing has changed
except that the headteacher has made it clear to Kerry that she's
moved nearer to permanent exclusion. Even this doesn't make
much difference. Part of Kerry is frightened at the thought of such a
punishment but another part will deal with the fear by attacking it
directly: 'Kick me out then! See if I care!' It's so easy to get herself
excluded. It's a much more familiar way of adapting than to stay
and live with the demands, the compromises, the anxieties, imperfections and sheer *ordinariness* of daily school life.

But the headteacher knows that young people need the security
of knowing where they stand. What this headteacher avoids doing,
however, is humiliating Kerry by demanding public apologies and
self-abasement in front of lots of adults. Instead the headteacher
meets with Kerry alone. Kerry emerges chastised but with dignity.
She writes a note to Miss Roberts. She and I continue to meet.

Our conversation is a delicate business. We have to find a way of
acknowledging and talking about Kerry's underlying neediness
(the lost world she yearns for) while also acknowledging and
respecting her 15-year-old ways of coping. So I listen to a lot of
bravado about what she and her friends get up to, how much they

drink and how much they hate the police before we've done enough of that and can risk moving on to something a bit different.

She announces that she's going to get a tattoo.

I stop myself from pointing out that she's actually too young to get one and ask instead what it will be.

She says it'll be a heart, encased with barbed wire, adding, 'With only a tiny bit of heart showing through!'

I ask whether anyone will notice the heart in the middle of so much barbed wire.

She pauses. 'You might. And some of my mates.'

I ask what she hopes we'll realise when we see the heart.

'That I'm all right really. That I do have feelings. That I do care about some things.'

'Such as?'

'Such as my friends and what happens to them.'

I hear this as Kerry also caring about what happens to *herself*. She agrees.

I say it must be hard to let people see the heart when it's been hurt so much.

She agrees again. 'Yeah, like when people mess me about.'

'People who are disappointing,' I suggest. 'People who promise things and then can't be what they've promised to be.'

She nods enthusiastically. 'Yeah! Like teachers…'

And we get on to Miss Roberts and how hurt Kerry feels that this teacher no longer seems to have time for her. She talks about how it was before, when Miss Roberts really seemed to understand things and seemed to think Kerry was great.

I think (but don't say) that Miss Roberts represents the parent Kerry has lost and that, at some point in the future, we'll need to talk more explicitly about Kerry's parents. The loss of her original relationship with them will underlie her current focus on Miss Roberts. Instead I ask what happened to change things with Miss Roberts and Kerry begins the long story of what led up to their split.

As time goes on, we'll explore this split from different angles, including whether Miss Roberts meant to be quite as persecutory as

Kerry experienced her being. In this way we'll try to assuage Kerry's hurt and find some way of helping her think about and, ultimately, accept the real Miss Roberts as opposed to the imaginary one with whom she currently fights. But for now it's enough for me to listen to the loss Kerry has experienced. Other young people bring different stories to counselling but underneath them there is usually an equivalent loss and a yearning which they've learned to hide in a variety of sometimes self-destructive or anti-social ways.

That yearning goes on into later life. What changes is the way we cope with it. Storr (1996) argues that gurus are attractive because they offer us a delusional system to live by. We no longer struggle with an objective, harsh reality but immerse ourselves in the narcissistic delusions of the guru, freed from personal choice and responsibility. I've worked with some young people whose fantasy life is extensive and, as told to me, much more exciting than the real life they avoid. I've listened to teachers talk about young people who 'just can't stop telling lies'. Harry Potter or Roald Dahl's Matilda (1988) are only two examples of the child-with-special-powers genre beloved of so many writers because it touches on something so important. 'If only I wish it often enough and fervently enough, then it might just come true! If only I had a magic wand…!' Young people commonly believe that *other* young people are having a wonderful life (supported by wonderful parents) which they themselves have been unfairly denied. So, if *only* I could marry a film star or become a pop star or a famous footballer or just a very rich person, all my troubles would be over! We remain fascinated by 'ideal' families such as the Kennedys, the Royal Family, the Von Trapps and a thousand celebrities but even more fascinated by the 'reality' of these people when it is gradually, relentlessly exposed in the press. The more the myth is shattered, the more vicariously fascinating it all becomes. Our own disillusionment is enacted through the lives of others.

I sit with Kerry, wishing that the school could offer her some opportunity to take responsibility for others. Many of her stories portray her as an heroic fighter for just causes. Needing a Valiant Knight, she becomes one herself. She tells Miss Roberts to fuck off on behalf of countless other Kerries whom she imagines are unable to do it for themselves.

Almost inevitably, she says she wants to work with children when she leaves school. The urge to protect children (and animals) is powerful in young people who have felt unprotected themselves. I'm reminded of another young person, Megan, who also wanted to work with children. Megan was sexually abused by her father (another kind of broken promise) but she protected people in a different way from Kerry. Megan did it by becoming depressed. Her voice was barely audible, her face impassive. At our first counselling session, she presented me with wrists which had been neatly, politely cut.

My work with Megan centred on helping her re-discover the voice she had effectively swallowed and the rage she had suppressed in order to protect others from its ferocity. By telling me her story, she could practise verbalising those feelings instead of denying them and then, when they became too difficult, taking them out on herself. Telling someone how you feel is a kinder strategy than cutting your wrists.

In a way, Kerry is an expert at verbalising how she feels. Unlike Megan, she shrieks it from the rooftops. And that gets her excluded. Megan was never excluded and was barely even noticed, but her struggle was just as great as those students who, like Kerry, do succeed in being noticed.

A school is made up of young people all finding different ways to tell their stories, to adapt to the reality into which they've emerged. Somehow schools have to be, in Winnicott's (1965a, p.148) famous phrase, 'good enough' for everyone. Whether they like it or not, schools provide a transitional mothering experience. Elsewhere, Winnicott (1965b) suggests that we need two kinds of mothering: the mothering of an 'object-mother' and of an 'environment-mother'. By 'object-mother', he means our original mother, the object of our immediate physical desires, the one who satisfies our emotional needs. By 'environment-mother' he means the one who takes care of our safety, who protects us, who provides us with an environment in which we can begin to explore. We need both kinds of mothering – mothering which can, of course, sometimes be provided by men. Young people unwittingly distinguish between the two kinds when they declare, 'This school's okay, I just hate Mr Bloggs!', or 'I hate everything about this school except for Mr Bloggs'.

I think Kerry's relationship with Miss Roberts is with an object-mother who, as Kerry discovers, *cannot* satisfy her need to be emotionally fed and held close in the way she desires. But her other relationship, which is just as important, is with the school more generally as an environment-mother. In meeting with Kerry when she returns from exclusion, the headteacher, for those 20 minutes, has to represent Kerry's need for someone who cares for her *and* someone who provides an environment with clear boundaries. Despite Kerry's wish for some of the lovely mothering she dreams of, it's important for the headteacher to be realistic with her. Schools don't always help young people in coming to terms with the dream and the reality when they trade on being the Best School with the Best Teachers and the Best Results. Young people know that the reality isn't like that (see Chapter 6). Sometimes they might like to believe it as much as the staff might, but they know it's not true and that disconcerts and aggravates. It's another example of the mismatch between the dream and the reality with which they've been wrestling all day. When the falseness comes from teachers, it stinks. I remember, in my first year as a teacher, managing to persuade a particular boy to do some work for once. Seeing what he'd done, I was so relieved that I praised him over and over again for his fabulous paragraph of writing. He sneered and, in the next lesson, did nothing.

Like most young people trying to work things out for themselves, Kerry has a top-of-the-range bullshit detector. One of the things which makes it possible for her to talk about something as personal as the loss of her lovely child's world is the obvious fact that she keeps turning up for sessions. And the reason she keeps turning up is that she hasn't had to deal with the additional disappointment of finding out that her counsellor, as well as Miss Roberts, cannot be her lovely object-mother. Her counsellor never promised to be in the first place.

I think I can help young people best when I am what I appear to be. I've worked with many counsellors starting to work in schools who have only been trained to work with consenting adults. That training, handed down from traditional psychoanalytic practice, supposes that the counsellor will say nothing about him or herself and will remain opaque. Questions to the counsellor will be deflected back as interesting insights into the questioner.

On the whole, this doesn't work for young people. It's weird. They've never met anyone behaving like this before. Many of them go away and simply don't come back. I'm not arguing for an unthinking relationship between adults and young people where power is eventually abused in the name of a more relaxed but unboundaried relationship. I am arguing for a quality of deliberate *realness* in relationships because, in my experience, most vulnerable young people cannot withstand a deliberately intensified transference relationship. In the film *Good Will Hunting* (Van Sant 1997) the boy makes mincemeat of various therapists, all sticking to their textbook formulas, before finding in the Robin Williams character a therapist prepared to engage in a two-way relationship between human beings. Williams doesn't abandon his role (or, I assume, stop having supervision) but he recognises that his young client needs him, above all else, to be authentic. Lomas (1987) and Yalom (2001) argue that the usefulness of a long and thorough training is that we can then *adapt* it to meet the needs of each differing client. Transference will occur at some level in all relationships anyway. We don't need to encourage it. What matters, they argue, is to be authentic.

I was the counsellor in a school at the same time as I was based in an adjoining building as the youth worker. So during school time I saw students for formal counselling in my youth centre office, surrounded by table tennis bats, snooker cues and photos on the wall of histrionic peers pulling faces. Then, in the evening, those same school students came back into the same office to buy sweets, read magazines and store their guitars.

When I began, the youth centre had only just been built on the school site. Before that, it had been a bedraggled building off the site where the youth workers regularly criticised the teachers in front of young people in order to gain favour. And at school the next day, the teachers reciprocated.

Once my dual role as counsellor and youth worker had begun there was quickly a showdown. I'd been involved in an incident in school where a boy had been rude to me and one of the teachers I was supporting who had given him a detention. When he then assumed he would come to the youth centre disco as though nothing had happened, I stopped him on the basis that I was the same person in school as I was in the youth centre and that respecting other people mattered wherever you were.

The other youth workers were outraged. This was a youth centre, not a school, they insisted. It was completely different. The youth centre management committee became involved and they, too, were horrified.

I can't remember how the incident was resolved – I know I lived to fight another day – but it marked the start of a changing relationship between the school and youth centre. As expectations about behaviour gradually became more consistent, the young people relaxed. The youth centre kept its distinct identity but the range of young people using it broadened and the sense of a hard-core of disaffected students in school (who had all previously monopolised the youth centre) diminished. I think what happened was that those young people stopped splitting their parent figures so readily into good or bad, saintly or devilish, and began to see them instead as ordinary adults doing different jobs. These parent figures were no longer so exciting, so *rude* about each other, but nor were they so disappointing.

As a counsellor in that setting I think it was a positive advantage to have both roles. I kept conversations and information from counselling completely separate when I talked to the same young people in school corridors or went with them on youth centre trips or cooked pancakes. But I was de-mystified. It became *normal* to talk about upsetting feelings with the counsellor and then, later that day, show him how to dance properly. It was 'safe', a word young people use to denote something both authentic and deserving of respect.

'School starts with a lot of promises but it just gets more and more disappointing,' says Kerry. I decide to tell her about the inclusion project I'm working for because the same criticism is levelled at us. In the eyes of some adults, we are Super-People with magic wands who will quickly make everything better. When we don't live up to that billing, we become Useless-People, barely able to break out of paper bags without help. Perhaps there's a connection, I wonder aloud to Kerry. Perhaps everything ends up being a bit of a disappointment when we've expected it to be so good? Perhaps it's not just school. Perhaps that's just how things are…?

We're meeting after Christmas, after that time of the year when childhood takes on an especially rosy glow and our nostalgic dreams are thoroughly tested by the realities of family life. Kerry reports having rowed on Boxing Day with her mum who, she says, hates her and keeps picking on her. She says she'd like to tell her mum to fuck off.

I set up two chairs: one for Kerry, one for her mum. I invite her to sit in the Kerry chair and say what she needs to say to her mum in the other chair.

Kerry does this.

I ask her to become her mum in the other chair and reply.

'I can't do that!'

But she agrees to try it.

I ask her, as her mum, what she has to say to the charges brought by Kerry.

Her mum vehemently defends herself.

I ask her, as her mum, whether it's true that she no longer cares about Kerry or whether it's just harder nowadays to show Kerry what she feels.

'I do care. You piss me off sometimes, though, Kerry. Badly! But you *are* my daughter and you always will be.'

Kerry comes back to being herself. 'So why d'you keep picking on me, then?'

And as her mother, she replies.

I let the conversation run for a minute. This kind of role reversal works as a reality-test for young people. In enabling Kerry to become briefly one of the voices stored in her head – in this case, her mother – she's obliged to confront a different reality from the slightly paranoid, defensive one in which she was immersing herself. This way, she has to see herself through someone else's eyes.

One of the characteristics of lovely, faraway worlds is that they are left over from a stage in our earliest development when, for a time, we believed we were omnipotent, controlling our mothers as extensions of ourselves. Little by little, as we grew up, we were forced to acknowledge the existence of other people who were separate from ourselves, people also exercising control over the world. Being able to reverse roles in this way is a good sign because it means Kerry can distinguish between her existence and that of other people. Being unable to do so would indicate that her internal psychological world was still worryingly under-developed with no differentiation between herself and other people.

I stop the conversation between Kerry and her mum. As a further reality-test, I ask Kerry to join me, away from the two chairs, in order to look at them and think about what has just gone on between the two people. For Kerry, this is like looking in a mirror: a technique much beloved of story writers where the protagonist extricates him or herself from a difficult situation and looks with detachment at what's really happening. Because, when we're able to do that, we often see ourselves differently. Realisations dawn.

Today Kerry sees herself through her mother's eyes and now through the eyes of an observer. 'I suppose my mum's all right really!'

We both laugh.

'She *so* annoys me though!'

We talk some more and sit back in our normal chairs. Because young people are often so preoccupied with what their parents *can't* be (the loss of their dream), they find it hard to make use of what their parents *can* be.

The bell is about to go when Kerry comments, 'I'm really hungry!'

As we walk back across the playground together, I'm left wondering how much our discussion has reminded her of a hunger which can never be satisfied merely by the breaktime canteen.

We continue our meetings and I continue to hope that she won't do or say anything to get herself excluded. But I keep my anxiety to myself and don't fall into the trap of prescribing solutions. To do that would be to imply that, if only Kerry could find a magic wand like mine, all would be well.

Her exams are approaching fast. Exams do funny things to young people. The majority redouble their efforts, working harder and spending less time with their friends. But for many, the exams are a horrible reminder of imminent separation from the transitional mother (school) and they have decidedly mixed feelings about this. For a few, exams are a brutal reality that they would do anything to avoid facing.

Kerry tells me that she may have to cancel our meetings if they clash with her exams.

8

Anger and identity

Dennis is the school caretaker. Dennis spends a lot of time going round repairing the things that have been damaged. He says he doesn't mind doing it but that Steve, the other caretaker, gets really fed up. It's the way some of them have no respect, Dennis says. Always breaking things. Treating the school like a pigsty. Most of them are all right though, he says. It's the parents' fault. The parents don't look after them properly. The parents should have to come in and see all the mess that he and Steve and the cleaners are expected to clear up every day.

He tells me in detail about one particularly gruesome example, discovered recently in a toilet, and also about how the flowerbed was getting used as a short cut to the maths block.

I comment that the flowerbed seems to be surviving now, thanks to Dennis's persistence and the little fence placed around it.

'Not before time,' he says, 'else I'd have been straight over to the headmaster with my notice!'

Dennis regularly threatens to do this but really as a way of signalling when he's feeling that he is being taken for granted. He knows that in a school there will, from time to time, be students. The students like Dennis. They're not so keen on Steve because they know Steve never really forgives them for the mess and for the things they vandalise. Steve scowls. Dennis smiles. They like Dennis.

His efforts pay off. Something broken and left publicly un-repaired in a school tends to get broken more and more emphatically as each day passes. Once it's repaired, there's at least a hesitation among students about breaking it again. It survives for longer. And when it's repaired yet again, there's a chance it will survive for even longer because breaking whatever somebody has obviously cared for gets harder. It's more personal. It leaves a more guilty feeling.

Not that the urge to break things goes away. If something is vulnerable or broken in a school – a wall panel, a plant, a display, a plastic bottle on the floor – there are students who don't step round it, hoping it will remain intact, worrying that something so fragile might break. Instead, they kick it in. Hard. Repeatedly. Until it's properly broken.

Its vulnerability is too much to bear. When they're clinging to the few things that they can still trust in themselves – their anger, their stubbornness, their defiance – it's unnerving to be reminded in corridors and classrooms of things vulnerable or broken. So they hurry to destroy the evidence.

If someone can be bothered to repair the damage, then that's up to them.

I'm talking with Dennis in the corridor while waiting for Karl to appear for his first counselling appointment. He and Aaron broke into the school two weeks ago, set off fire extinguishers in the Humanities block and wrote 'FUCK' in very large letters on a blackboard.

The next morning, Aaron boasted to friends about what he and Karl had done and later, while Dennis was busy repairing the damage, the headteacher spoke in assembly about the break-in. He asked anyone who knew anything to tell a member of staff. So two students, who'd heard Aaron talking, told their head of year at breaktime. Aaron was summoned to the headteacher's office where he admitted what he'd done. He said breaking into the school had been Karl's idea.

Three hours later, once the police had finished interviewing them, Karl and Aaron were excluded from school.

They came back two weeks later. Aaron's dad said his son wouldn't be going out for the rest of term and would be working with him every Saturday to pay for the damage.

Karl's mum said she no longer knew what to do with him. She said he'd changed. He was never at home in the evenings and never told her anything. The headteacher suggested that counselling might give Karl a chance to talk about things. Karl shrugged his indifference but agreed to give it a go.

Now he ambles along the corridor towards where Dennis and I are talking. Dennis sees him, mutters something under his breath about culprits and slopes off.

I smile and shake hands with Karl, whom I've never met before. He offers me his blankest look.

We go into the counselling room and sit down. I explain who I am, what counselling is and isn't, how confidential I can and can't be and what will happen at the end of our session. His show of utter indifference is making me feel nervous: probably the same feeling that Karl himself is hiding. I imagine he's waiting for me to ask about the break-in. He'll mumble a few things about breaking into school not being such a big deal and then, according to the script he's used to, I'll put him right about burglary, vandalism, owning up to things, peer pressure, talking to his mum, the importance of education, the seriousness of crime and the inevitability of prison for persistent young offenders. He'll remain blank, will not disagree with anything I say and will leave with the faintest of smirks on his face. I will later report to the headteacher that things don't look good.

Instead, we draw a family tree.

Karl lives with his mum, two younger sisters and step-dad. His sisters are six and eight years younger than Karl and are the children of his mum and step-dad. Both his mum and step-dad have parents who come over to the house regularly. Karl says he doesn't know anything about his own dad and doesn't want to.

We continue with the family tree, putting in uncles and aunts and cousins. Karl keeps his air of indifference but has relaxed slightly, realising that all he has to do is tell me who's who. I draw the family tree. He speaks about his half-sisters and cousins with mild affection and leans closer to check that I've not made mistakes.

I say we've made a good beginning and suggest we meet again. I say I'd like to hear next time about some of the things which get on his nerves. He nods ruefully, confirming that there are plenty of those, and agrees to meet again.

The next time we meet he tells me plenty: about teachers, friends, enemies, his mum, step-dad, people at Army Cadets. With five minutes to go, I point out that he hasn't said anything about his dad.

'There's nothing to say!'

I ask where his dad lives.

'How should I know?'

'Does your mum know?'

'She never mentions him.'

'Do you ask?'

'No!'

'Because...?'

'Because I'm not interested. He's nothing to do with me. If he'd wanted to know me he would have got in touch years ago. But he doesn't and I certainly don't want to know about him. All he's ever brought my family is trouble!'

I ask if that's what his mum says.

'She's told me what he's like. He's a loser. He left Mum as soon as he knew she was pregnant and when he found out that he had a son he couldn't even be bothered to visit. He was down the pub!'

The bell is about to go for the end of the lesson and we've done a lot. I state the obvious: 'Sounds like you wouldn't want to have anything to do with him.' Karl's already told me this but it gives him an opportunity to tell me again, to put back his I-don't-care-about-my-dad defence in case anything regretful or questioning has been stirred by our conversation. I assume Karl keeps feelings like those under 24-hour surveillance.

'To tell you the truth, I wouldn't spit on my dad's grave!'

The bell has gone.

'See you next time, Karl.'

He thinks for a moment. 'Yeah, okay.'

We exchange blokeish goodbyes and I close the door behind him.

There are a significant number of young people like Karl who have no conscious memory at all of one parent, usually of their father. Their fathers either left before they were born or left in the very first years of their life. Inevitably, the family then re-grouped and the absent father came to represent a bad time in everyone's lives. He was a loser, Karl says.

But once the child of that man reaches adolescence, he or she has a difficult job to do in trying to make sense of who they are when one part of who they are has always been identified so firmly with something bad, untrustworthy, uncaring and unloving. Try as he will to identify himself only with his mother's family, Karl knows that part of who he is comes from his father. So when he's angry or vengeful or feels like hurting someone it's easy for him to make the link... Perhaps I *am* bad? Perhaps the things people say when they're fed up with me are true? Perhaps I am my father's son and always will be? Perhaps *I'm* the loser?

Part of the job of a counsellor is to re-construct with the young person a sense of this absent father which is more balanced than the previously accepted and firmly fixed story of a bad man, a loser. So we talk about the first years of the young person's life: what they know, what they've heard and, most importantly, what they *imagine*. We think back to the very beginning, to their mum and dad meeting. We wonder what attracted them to each other, what she saw in him, what his good qualities were. We wonder about the pregnancy: whether he was a coward who didn't care or whether he just got scared; whether he had a father for himself, whether he had any confidence in himself, whether he was good or bad at showing his feelings. We wonder how he might really have felt inside when he knew he had a son...

There are all sorts of questions. The young person supplies some information, handed down by the family or observed in photographs. But the *imagined* information is the most important because that is the story most alive in the young person's mind, the story that matters, the one about motives and feelings rather than just events. We all construct autobiographies for ourselves. Usually our stories can change, assimilating and adapting to new information and new perspectives. But for Karl, his story remains static, refusing to accommodate anything which threatens its simplicity. Winnicott (1986, p.141) writes: 'The most aggressive and therefore the most dangerous words in the languages of the world are to be found in the assertion I AM.'

But young people who cling to a simple story like Karl's do so for good reasons. His 'Dad' story is safe. It's about values with which he can identify. It's about loyalty (fathers *should* stick by their children), about the importance of demonstrating love (fathers *should* show their children that they care) and it's about not being soft on crime (fathers who let their children down *should* be punished). Karl knows what he's talking about. His harshness is indicative of his certainty.

Children turn into adolescents when they finally realise that the world and their parents are more complex than they ever supposed. So, in Karl's case, when one parent remains wholly 'bad', that developmental process gets stuck. Fourteen-year-old Karl then attacks his school for not being as 'good' as it should be in the same spirit as four-year-old Karl might have smashed up a toy which wouldn't do as he wanted. The older Karl still hasn't got used to schools and parents being a mixture of good intentions and eventual imperfections. To him, it doesn't make sense. It doesn't fit the story. To him, his father is a loser. As simple as that.

'A total waste of space,' he repeats, the next time we meet.

His behaviour has enacted something important, however. Young people who vandalise or break into schools are attacking the very thing which is trying to support and nurture them, the same thing which is trying and often failing, which can never provide all that they need, which lets them down. For Karl, this resonates with his own feeling about fathers. What Karl did to the school expressed something of his clumsy, muddled rage towards a father who isn't what Karl wants him to be and whom he can't confront, even imaginatively. It also expressed something of Karl's *need*. Why else break into your own school? Cool kids stay away from school as much as possible. What Karl and Aaron did was to get back *inside* their school, almost as if they were looking for something or needing to finish something off. (And they are not the only ones with unfinished school business, as the surge in Internet reunions demonstrates.)

Phillips (1994) writes that people come for counselling 'because the way they are remembering their lives has become too painful; the stories they are telling themselves have become too coercive and restrictive'. The aim of therapy, he writes, is 'to produce a story of the past…that makes the past available, as a resource to be thought about rather than a persecution to be endlessly re-enacted' (p.69). Although he'd be unable to explain it in these terms, Karl keeps agreeing to meet with me.

I ask how his mum and step-dad are. Karl's fondness for his step-dad is evident but is founded on the fact of his step-dad not being his dad, the loser.

'He's stuck by my mum through everything, even when she was depressed. He says I'm the son he never had. He says he's always treated me as his own. He says for my birthday we're going to Center Parcs and I can take a friend.'

I listen before asking about his original birthday.

He was born in the local hospital. There are no photos.

I ask what people say about when he was born.

'Nothing!'

I ask what he imagines it was like.

'How should I know? I was busy!'

We laugh.

'Probably my nan and grandad came to visit,' he says. 'And Aunty Pam, Mum's friend. She says the first two words I ever said in my life were "get" and "lost"!'

'Because she thinks you're stroppy?'

'Because she *knows* I'm stroppy!'

Suddenly the story of Karl, the peaceable, home-loving son, is wobbling. 'You've probably needed to say "Get lost!" a lot,' I suggest.

He thinks.

'It's really important,' I tell him, 'to be able to say "Get lost!", so that people don't muck you around. So that they listen. I imagine people do listen when you're telling them something important?'

Karl looks puzzled. 'Not always.'

'Like when?'

'Like at school when people are pissing me off. They don't listen. They're only interested in what they're doing.'

'How would you prefer them to be?'

'Proper mates,' Karl says. 'Sticking by each other. When one of my mates gets into trouble I always stick by them!'

'Because you're a friend?'

He nods.

'Aaron told the headteacher that breaking into the school was your fault.'

'Aaron's a tosser! He grassed on me!'

'Maybe standing by someone isn't simple. Maybe he got scared.'

'How d'you mean?'

'Well, we might *aim* to stand by our friends and we might want to, but, when it comes to it, we sometimes get scared. We're not always as brave as we wish we could be. That doesn't make someone a bad friend, just because they can't be brave all the time. It makes them normal.'

Karl thinks about this. He'll continue the debate and, if he insists on his old point of view, I'll back off again because we're really talking about his father. I avoid making that explicit. Telling

Karl what to think about his dad would be as prescriptive and unhelpful as the original story he told himself about his dad the loser. It would shift nothing. Rose (2001, p.45) warns against interpreting a young person's defence 'without taking account of the anxiety against which it is defending'.

As the weeks go by, however, things are loosening up. He concedes that people's opinions can change and that his mum must have cared about his dad once. In thinking about how hard it must have been for his mum to be on her own with a baby, he concedes that things might have been difficult for his dad as well. He remembers from somewhere that his dad didn't get on with either of his own parents. We talk then about the possibility of his dad being lonely and whether his dad might have pretended to be more confident than he sometimes felt...

All of this is giving back to Karl possibilities for himself. It becomes much easier for him to acknowledge a mixture of feelings in himself if he can conceive of others feeling similarly mixed. And when he can be a mixture of feelings, he can relax a little. He no longer has to fight to hold on to simplicities which were becoming more and more untenable as he got older. The dad he's now creating in his head is a more useful dad: more rounded, more emotionally accessible, more diverse. He's still an *idea* rather than a physical presence but he's an idea of a dad that Karl can carry around inside himself.

Winnicott's (1965b, pp.140–152) idea of a false self ('I hate my dad') developing to protect a true self ('I don't know who my dad is and I hate not knowing') is helpful in relation to Karl. Winnicott writes: 'When the false self becomes exploited and treated as real there is a growing sense in the individual of futility and despair.' I think this is true of many young people and is what Karl's breaking into school was really a way of expressing. In the long run, being excluded from school isn't half as bad as being excluded from having a real dad.

As another man in his life of whom Karl is trying to make sense, I try to be reliable and warm-hearted, persistent and open to suggestion. Like Dennis the caretaker, I keep trying to repair the damage and the more I persist (along with his teachers and the other people supporting Karl), the less inclined Karl is to re-open the wound and make it bleed again. 'I hate my dad' was never entirely true and it hurt to keep saying it because it also meant 'I hate part of myself'.

His mum has been to a parents' evening and Karl's form tutor tells me that his mum was saying that Karl's behaviour at home is worse. He's now openly rude and has started refusing to do what his step-dad says. His mum is worrying that counselling might be making things worse, but was pleased to hear from the form tutor that Karl seems more involved in school and is working well in some subjects.

I think my own thoughts. A number of things can happen at this point in Karl's life. His behaviour at home may be part of a balancing-up, whereby, if his dad is no longer the Loser, his mum and step-dad can no longer be the Martyrs. They may now be getting some of what Karl always reserved for his dad.

Like other young people, Karl may decide to trace and even meet up with his father as part of making further sense of himself. He may start idealising his father, in which case his mum and step-dad are in for a torrid time. But my hope is that he continues to address these things from the safety of our counselling relationship.

So when Karl doesn't arrive for his next appointment, I check that he's in school and not ill. We've been booking appointments from week to week, so we now have no appointment booked for the following week or beyond. His English teacher confirms that he was in her lesson and was working hard. Karl doesn't find me to apologise for missing the session.

I wait.

Nothing happens.

Two weeks later, just as I'm beginning to think I must write to him, I bump into Karl in the corridor. He explains that he forgot our session and is sorry. I ask if he wants to make an appointment.

He hesitates. 'Can we give it a break for now? I don't think I really need to come at the moment.'

My counsellor's instinct is to have Proper Endings where people evaluate the work they've done in counselling and say a thorough goodbye, practising for the times in their life when they will need to end and make sense of relationships. But for some young people it doesn't work like that. They've already had enough. It's no big deal and no avoidance. They're ready to fly. They haven't got time to say endless goodbyes.

I let Karl go.

He smiles at me.

I swallow my feelings.

Weeks later, I see him at the far end of the corridor, some friends around him, teasing and joking with Dennis.

Anger and envy

A lot of *slagging off* goes on. In playgrounds and corridors, on pavements and dancefloors there's the daily cry of 'Slag!', 'Whore!', 'Dog!', 'Bitch!'. There's the daily irony of boys constantly calling each other 'Wanker!'. Young people can be slagged off for being sexually active or sexually inactive. They can be slagged off for being lazy or hard-working, for being young, affectionate, eccentric, gay, confident, wrong, attached, successful, tall, small or different in any way.

'Stop slagging me off!'

'I wasn't slagging you off!'

'So what *were* you doing?'

'Nothing!'

'Oh yeah?'

'Yeah! Look, I *wasn't* slagging you off, okay? If I wanted to slag you off, I'd do it to your face!'

Where I work, it's called slagging off, but there's an equivalent phrase everywhere because the activity is so endemic to young people. Slagging people off – cursing or verbally attacking or criticising other people behind their backs – is, for some young people and in some contexts, a way of life, a constant hostile undercurrent, more or less hostile depending on the situation. And when that hostility is at its most intense or is most calculated to hurt, feuds and fights break out which in schools can result in the protagonists being excluded as teachers struggle to know what else to do with such apparently pointless behaviour.

'She called me a slag, so I hit her!'

'He insulted my family, so I told him where to go!'

'They were getting at me, so I walked out!'

It goes on and on. Some of it is simply one person ascribing his or her own unacknowledged anxiety to another person, 'You're thick… You're always running to your mum… You're such a wanker… You're two-faced!', but I think that denigration ('slagging people off') is also a way in which young people cope with envy.

Among professionals working with young people, little is said or written about envy, yet envy is a constant, core experience in young people's lives, expressed particularly through the denigration of others, the constant undercurrent which sours many young people's experience of school.

It's easy for young people to believe that everyone else is having a much better time than they are. Other people seem to have more friends and to be more cool. They're more successful, more attractive, more clever or more funny. Their parents are much more understanding and appreciative. Things come easily to other people. Other people don't worry about things. Melanie Klein's (1957) contention is that envy is intrinsic even to babies who, in as much as they experience a mother providing for them, also experience her as necessarily (and deliberately) withholding whenever she's *not* around to satisfy their hunger or need. Babies therefore envy their mothers for having more than those mothers seem prepared to share.

By the time the baby has become a teenager, however, the sense of 'mother' has dispersed into many other everyday relationships. Teachers and other parent figures pick up the role. In the eyes of young people, for example, the police are always discriminating against *us*. To young people, teachers are always more interested in *the others*. Salzberger-Wittenberg (1970, p.117) writes:

> The situation of being dependent, or being a learner, may become quite intolerable because feelings of inferiority provoke such hostility in relation to the person who is in the position of parent or teacher. Every gift becomes suspect as if it was designed to show off the superiority of the giver.

Teachers feel the hostility of their envious, disparaging students: 'She's a crap teacher... She only teaches the ones she likes... She's not interested in us... We've never learned anything from her!' Teachers have envious feelings of their own towards students who get away with misbehaving in ways that teachers can't and who have much more care lavished on them than teachers can ever expect for themselves. Teachers despair of the way students are never satisfied but always expect more, while the unconscious belief of students is that the teachers have much more than they are ever prepared to give.

For most young people, however, the target of their fiercest envy is 'mother's' other children, the ones she seemingly produced because she wasn't prepared to give herself entirely to those she already had. As they get older, young people attack, denigrate, slag off these other 'children' in classrooms and youth centres, on buses and street corners.

Lindsay had been excluded from school for slagging people off: for her constant, niggly undermining of other students as well as for her public confrontations with staff. Officially, she had been 'disrupting lessons and preventing other students from working'.

As if to warn me that she was not as she seemed, the very first thing she told me about herself was, 'I'm a natural blonde!' Her hair was dyed jet black.

She ranted about the awfulness of everyone: her teachers and all but a few fellow students. They were all stupid, superficial, dishonest, *childish*. She herself wasn't any of these things. 'And I hate my sister!'

I asked about her mum and dad.

'They're not important!' she said, adding that her mum could be 'extremely childish'.

Our sessions would begin with a rant about the awfulness of her week and the people she was forced to deal with. Little by little, we would edge towards the flip side of her hostility: the affection she felt for some people, her protective feelings towards children and the way she felt close to her sister occasionally.

'But *only* occasionally.'

We talked about her 'childish' mother who favoured her sister and had absolutely no idea what Lindsay was really like.

One day, she told me about a dream she'd had. In the dream she had a fight with another girl in a tennis court and badly beat up the other girl. She then found that the gates of the tennis court were locked and they couldn't get out.

I asked who'd locked the gates.

'I don't know.'

'What happened next?'

'I don't know. We were just *in* there.'

I asked how it felt, being in there.

For once, she had nothing to say. She looked perplexed. It seemed that the dream had ended as Lindsay had woken up, still inside the tennis court with her injured rival.

I asked how she would have liked to change the dream.

'I'd have liked someone to come and let me out!'

I asked who.

'My friends.'

I understood that I was probably one of the 'friends' she would like help from. I'd been allowed to see how it felt to be stuck in a tennis court, full of rivalry and fighting and guilt, and I was being given permission to help Lindsay get out. We said nothing about rival sisters, unfair mothers or childishness, but we had a beginning now, an implicit understanding that Lindsay wasn't the omnipotent adult she pretended to be. She needed help to get out of the feelings which trapped her. I think these included her feelings of envy towards her mother and sister.

Slagging other people off all the time implied that Lindsay was above them. It made her unpopular. The more she slagged other people off, the more wonderful she set herself up to be. Coren (1997) writes about young people's need to denigrate ('You're rubbish!') and the grandiosity ('I'm great!') which often accompanies it: 'Part of the grandiosity is based on a profound denial; what is denied is one's own helplessness, incompetence, and loss of parental support or encouragement' (p.16). It's tempting for young people to believe that such vulnerabilities are now behind them (or ought to be) because now they can have sex, stay out late, drink lots of alcohol and be physically strong. The fear, the knowledge of their continuing limitations and frailties, is denied (or projected onto others). Josephine Klein (1987) describes this as a split developing between 'the grandiose self' and 'the wretched self' (pp.222–223).

Anna was another student whose depression was the result of struggling to manage such a split. She had taken an overdose and then been off school, recovering at home. Just as Lindsay had done, Anna described herself to me in our first session as 'a control freak'. She wore lots of brave make-up and, like Lindsay, had lots of sharp words to say about other people. She talked a lot. Talking seemed to be a way in which she hid herself from certain feelings. For while she continued to be charming, funny and articulate, there were no silences in our conversation. Silences are terrifying for some young people. Being silent feels like being alone, being invisible, naked, worthless.

'I'm afraid of having nothing to say,' she admitted.

I asked what that was like.

Tears welled up. 'I have good days and bad days,' she said, starting to cry. 'When things go wrong, I crumble.'

For years, she had lived alone with her mother. Then, when she was eight, her mother had married again and had two more children. When she was 11, Anna had been sent to a boarding school from which she was permanently excluded two years later.

'I hated it so much! It was such a dump! They couldn't control me. The teachers were scared of me! Mind you, I was *evil*. I was really bad with people I didn't like. I used to hit them. I broke one boy's nose. There were just three people in the whole school that I liked and I'd do anything for them. If one of them was in trouble, I was in there, straight away, sorting it out for them. I wasn't bothered what they'd done. All the teachers hated me because I was so mouthy but I didn't care!' She paused for breath.

I imagined Anna taking out on the parent and sibling figures at boarding school all her feelings about a mother sharing herself with a new husband and two new children. I asked about her mother.

Anna said she felt angry. And guilty. She felt bad for causing her mum so much hassle. She often made her mum cry but that just made Anna herself feel worse. 'Then I feel like I'm a really bad person. I go up to my room and stay there for hours, feeling really bad.'

I asked whether that was because she imagined no one would want to know a really bad person.

She nodded through fresh tears.

Our work would try to bring together Anna's 'grandiose self' and her 'wretched self', to understand the relationship between them and the cause of their split, stemming, no doubt, from the earlier part of her life and Anna's changed relationship with her mother. It seemed that whenever her grandiose self broke down or started to feel the effects of its hostility towards other people, hurting them and isolating Anna from them, her wretched self then appeared, full of guilt and self-loathing.

In the weeks that followed, we talked a lot about her mother and how things had been in the early part of her life. She and her mum had been very close, she said. Like sisters. They'd stuck up for each other because they were on their own, Anna's dad having left before she was born and her mum's parents having disowned their daughter. It had all gone wrong once her mum had started going to evening classes and doing exams. Then she'd got a job and then she'd met the man to whom she was now married.

We had discovered the time in her life where Anna had got hurt and where it was still hurting; the time where she had felt worthless, wretched, as if she no longer counted, as if her mum no longer had time for her; the time where she had started going up to her room and staying there to avoid her mum. Going back to these memories was painful but necessary in order for Anna to speak her feelings honestly and be listened to for the first time. Originally these feelings had been expressed through her changing behaviour at home: anger covering for hurt, tears covering for envy. Her real feelings had become twisted and hidden, the more shameful as she got older. Her grandiose self had developed simply as a way of keeping this wretchedness at bay.

Anna and Lindsay each kept a few people in their lives whom they didn't slag off but who had their undying admiration: the three chosen ones at Anna's boarding school, for example. There's a simple relationship between idealisation and denigration. If, for some reason, people can't be denigrated, either because they're already disadvantaged in some obvious way or because they have to be retained as allies, then those people have to be idealised instead as the most fantastic friends, relatives or lovers anyone could ever wish for. There's no middle ground.

'Why can't I stop feeling like this?' Michelle implored me at our first counselling session. 'I love him *so* much but I'm really afraid that if I keep going on like this it'll spoil everything between us!' For three weeks, she'd got stuck with the same question. Her fantastic, idealised boyfriend, for all his many qualities and for all the strength and determination of her love for him, wasn't perfect. He noticed other girls. This tortured Michelle but she wouldn't allow herself to feel angry or even disappointed with him. It was her fault, not his. She ought to be able to accept that he looked at other girls sometimes...but she couldn't...but she loved him *so* much...but she couldn't stop thinking about it. She was stuck, denying utterly the envious, hostile feelings she felt towards her boyfriend, not only for fancying other girls, but also for having had girlfriends before Michelle.

When such an idealised relationship can't be sustained, some young people retreat to the shelter of cynicism. Matthew had a reputation for cynically putting people down, so I was surprised when he made an appointment to see me because there are plenty of boys who hide their wish for what a counsellor offers by denigrating those who take up the offer.

He wasn't getting on with his parents. They were only interested in his brother, he said. They had no idea about anything to do with Matthew's school or his friends or fashion or 'what things are like nowadays'. He wanted to leave home, he said, and his parents wanted him to leave as well because of how he behaved with them.

I asked about that.

'I'm not a very nice person to live with,' he said. 'I swear a lot and I beat my brother up quite a bit. But *they* do things which annoy me as well!'

However resistant they may appear to be, young people who come willingly for counselling do so because something doesn't feel right (Phillips 1994). I think Matthew's cynicism at school and his behaviour at home, however justifiable they may or may not have been, were actually hurting him. He was hurt that his parents seemed unsympathetic to him and more interested in his brother. He was also hurt by having to portray himself as the uncaring son.

I asked who in the world would know what to do in Matthew's situation. Who would know what it was like?

He thought for a moment. 'Morrissey!'

At the time, Morrissey was an important pop star. I asked Matthew to tell me all the things he thought were good and that he admired about Morrissey. As he spoke, I wrote down the words and phrases on a piece of paper: brave, not scared of what people think, caring, good at standing up for beliefs, loyal, prepared to be different, able to talk about feelings, an individual, kind, determined, truthful, prepared to work hard, gentle, able to speak out about things which are unfair...

When Matthew had finished, I gave him the piece of paper and pen and asked him to write 'I am' in front of all the things he knew were also true about *himself.*

He looked at the list and wrote something.

He looked up. 'Shit!' A big smile spread across his face. He wrote some more. 'That's amazing!'

I asked him to read aloud to me all the sentences now beginning with 'I am'.

Uncertainly at first, he did so. When he'd finished, he stared at the page, hardly daring to look up, still shaking his head with surprise.

Eventually he looked up and sighed. 'So there!'

'So there!' I echoed. 'Not bad, eh?'

We met a few more times to consolidate what had happened. Matthew had allowed me to meet the person behind his behaviour. Having experienced this person as acceptable, even likeable, he'd given himself more choices for the future because he no longer had to punish himself by deliberately becoming all the things he was accused of being: the bad, the uncaring, the unfeeling son. He and I knew that he was all right, really.

Sometimes young people like Matthew, Michelle, Anna and Lindsay protect themselves with a posse of similarly anxious friends. In every school there are a few students whose main business seems to be organising others into nervous groups and sub-groups, in-groups and out-groups. These students never rest. They keep slagging people off, mocking, criticising and laughing. There is considerable fall-out from their feuding because someone is always in tears or retaliating. Parents arrive in Reception. Teachers call meetings to try and unpick who has said what to whom, whether they really meant it and why they said it, whether or not the people involved can agree to put it behind them and move on.

Often they can't. They say sorry in front of the teacher but with glowering eyes and unconcealed scorn. The inquests start in the corridor immediately afterwards: 'I don't care! Next time she says that to me I'm going to beat the crap out of her!' or, 'If he comes near me again I'm going straight to the headmaster!' The feud continues.

I remember working with Polly and her friends who all came to see me at their teacher's suggestion because they'd fallen out with Nicola. Polly's mum had died. Polly had returned to school quite quickly and, not knowing what else to do, her friends had formed an exclusion zone around her, policed by themselves. Polly was to be treated with kid gloves. Everyone was to look suitably mournful at the mention of Polly and everyone was to be *nice* to her. After all, 'How would you like it if *your* mum had died?'

Nicola's crime was that she'd allegedly commented to someone outside their friendship group that Polly was 'just loving all the attention'. Word got back, which gave the friends, especially Saff, the group's organiser and would-be leader, a perfect excuse to excommunicate Nicola. Not only was Nicola no longer allowed to go around with them or go near Polly, but everyone else in the year group was encouraged to despise Nicola. Some refused to work or sit with her in lessons.

Nicola fought back, trying to persuade some of them that she hadn't said it or hadn't meant it like that. She got angry. She cried. She missed a few days' school. She beseeched the others to believe her. Then she said she hated Saff. She persuaded her long-time friend, Sally, to go into a neutral corner. This irked Saff because it meant Saff's power was no longer absolute.

They sat in a messy circle in my room, Saff seething with righteous indignation, Nicola staring hopelessly at the floor, Sally uncomfortably beside her. The others, including Polly, were embarrassed and tried to look as if this was nothing to do with them.

I think the underlying issue for the group was about getting attention. They actually envied Polly. I suspect Nicola had spoken what everyone else was thinking but trying not to think. They were genuinely frightened by what had happened to Polly and all felt sorry for her but they were also intrigued and envious of her experience. They all secretly wished that they could have the quality of attention now afforded to Polly. A mother who dies too soon becomes a more perfect mother in everyone's eyes than the ones left alive who plough on every day, organising packed lunches, chasing homework, arguing about bed times and always getting older. Polly's mother was now a saint and Polly was lucky to have a saint for a mother when everyone else had to put up with such ordinary ones.

'We're here because we don't want to go round with Nicola any more,' announced Saff, 'and she's been slagging us off, telling teachers that we're being mean to her!'

'That's because you are!' Nicola said. 'You know you are and I don't know how you can say that, Saff, because how would you like it if no one was talking to you? I said I was sorry for what I said but I didn't mean anything against Polly. What do you expect me to say?'

Saff looked superior.

One of her allies joined in. 'You shouldn't have said what you said, Nicola. Her mum's *dead*! I just don't know how you could have said that!'

Sally spoke meekly, 'I don't agree with what Nicola said either, but she's said she's sorry.'

'Yeah?' Saff pounced. 'But *is* she, though? I mean, why would she say that in the first place if she didn't mean it? God, I mean, Nicola, we don't go round criticising *you* for wanting attention all the time or for expecting us to listen when your bloody *gerbil's* died!'

I decided to intervene before the row got worse and Nicola lost faith in me. 'Let's come back to the discussion,' I suggested. 'I want to hear about your mum, Polly, and about what happened.'

There was a pause. Polly looked sheepish.

'She probably doesn't want to talk,' Saff said. 'Do you?'

Polly said a little, about her mum having cancer and dying and how her dad cried at the funeral but she couldn't cry until afterwards and how quiet it seemed at home now.

The other girls were silent. They nodded supportively. I encouraged Polly to tell as much as she felt able. The rules were different now. We'd left behind the fight between Saff and Nicola and were concentrating on what had really provoked it. I asked how other people felt about their mothers at the moment, what the good and bad things were and what it would be like if their mothers weren't around.

The room suddenly came alive with talking. I suggested we go round, one at a time, so that everyone had a turn to speak and be listened to. When it was her turn, Nicola said she couldn't imagine losing her mum because she loved her so much, even though they weren't getting on at the moment. She said she felt really sad for Polly and couldn't imagine what it must be like for her.

Polly looked quietly pleased.

When the last person had spoken there was a sense of relief. They'd each had some attention. Some of them had wept and something of their investment in Polly's story had been implicitly acknowledged: their fear but also their interest in the idea of mothers dying and their concern about whether their own mothers were the best, as good as Polly's.

I asked whether we needed to go back to the original discussion or whether that didn't really matter so much. They nodded their agreement that it didn't matter so much now.

Saff felt obliged to say, 'I still don't think it was right what you said, Nicola.'

Again, Nicola said she was sorry.

I wound the session up and they went out with the bell, talking about PE kit and whether they were going to take part in PE, their next lesson.

I felt confident that Nicola's faux pas would be forgiven and that the group would move on. My concern was how to support Saff because, without Nicola to persecute and probably feeling exposed by the sincerity of our discussion, there was a danger that Saff would quickly cover up by finding a new target for the group to slag off.

It was hard to catch her alone. Eventually I found her in the canteen, on her way from the food counter to re-join the rest of the group, busily eating their lunches at tables. I thanked her for her contribution to our discussion and for her kindness in looking after Polly.

She seemed surprised and pleased. 'That's okay!'

I asked how Nicola was getting on.

She squirmed. 'Okay, I suppose. She's going round with us again.'

I asked her to let me know if there were ways in which I could help in the future.

She nodded. 'Actually I've been thinking of coming to see you... If that's okay?'

I said it was fine, it would be good to see her. Quickly, we made an appointment.

I wasn't surprised. Groups have often come to see me about something ostensibly concerning all of them when really they've each wanted to come and see me alone. They each have their own story to tell about unfair parents and pain-in-the-arse siblings. In one sense, feuds and fights are just a way of getting attention. What some young people miss and long for is an intimacy they feel they've lost with their mothers, either because they're now older and that relationship is more complex, or because they feel their behaviour has turned their mothers against them. Young people in Saff's position are keen to make changes but they're stuck. Paranoia is an exhausting and unhappy business. It's important to know that someone likes them even though their behaviour is making them seem so unlikeable. They're delighted when someone notices the good things about them because they know those good things *are* there and it hurts when people never seem to notice. When someone appeals to their kindness, the very thing that their constant denigration of others seemed to preclude, they melt.

Although many of them play hard to get, I think young people appreciate the fact that someone *hasn't* given up the chase. If their assumption as babies was that their 'mother' withheld her favours because she was no longer interested, their experience as young people can be that mother *figures* are interested and are persistent, however difficult the young person may be making things. The chasing-up of recalcitrant young people is never time wasted. It may not achieve its immediate aim of collecting the homework, finding out where they've been or resolving the dispute, but it achieves the much longer-term aim of beginning to correct a misapprehension.

Anger, violence and empathy

The only doubt was whether he'd kicked the boy's head. Liam said he hadn't but two girls who were coming out of another classroom at the same time were sure that they had seen Liam kick the boy's head when the boy was lying on the ground. What wasn't in any doubt was that Liam had gone up to the boy in the first place and punched him in the face. He'd then punched him several more times, breaking his nose.

Liam agreed that this had happened. He said he hadn't actually kicked the boy's head but that, in any case, the boy deserved it and he'd do it again. Any day. He wasn't bothered. It was the boy's fault for giving him dirty looks.

Liam was permanently excluded from the school and spent several weeks at home, waiting to find out what would happen next. After the police had gone, other professionals came round to talk with Liam and his mother, including a school re-integration worker whose job was to help make arrangements for his continuing education. The plan was for him to begin at a new school, provided that the new school would have him and provided that he was prepared to abide by its rules, which included a strict uniform, no swearing and no fighting.

Liam, his mother and the re-integration worker visited the new school to look round. In his office, the headteacher said he needed assurances from Liam that he would respect other students and staff and wouldn't be involved in any fighting. He said the school didn't have to take him if Liam wasn't prepared to co-operate.

Liam ducked further into his football scarf.

'Do you want to come to this school, Liam?'

He nodded.

His mother said he wanted to make a fresh start.

The headteacher explained that the school had a counsellor. A condition of joining the school would be that Liam saw the counsellor every week for the first couple of months. This would help him to settle in and would mean that, if there were any difficulties, he would have someone in school to talk with and get help from.

Liam said he didn't need help from a counsellor. He was fine.

The headteacher explained that this wasn't a punishment but a positive opportunity for Liam. He said that because of the seriousness of what had happened in Liam's last school he couldn't take any chances. Liam had to make a decision about starting and about seeing the counsellor as part of the deal.

Liam agreed to give it a try.

Kitted out in his new uniform, he started school the following week by hitting a boy with a speech difficulty in his new tutor group. Intrigued by Liam, the boy had asked to borrow his ruler. Liam had told him to fuck off. He had then hit the boy on the side of the head with the ruler, deliberately using the sharp edge.

Knowing that Liam was coming to see me as a condition of joining the school, I was wary. The chances of making a difference or even of making a relationship at all with him seemed slight. It's extremely difficult for young people to trust someone they've been forced to see and when a 14-year-old's behaviour towards others is so heartless, it suggests a degree of emotional and psychological damage which it would be hard for any school to repair. His file described a boy who, since the age of five, had never been able to make friends and who had been involved several times in acts of violence towards other students. Liam had never had a proper psychiatric assessment. Evidently it had been suggested when he was eight, after he'd threatened another boy with a cricket bat, but there was a letter in the file from his mother, angry at the suggestion that her son was 'mad' and refusing to let him be seen by anyone.

The headteacher told me about the recent incidents. It sounded as if Liam had felt nothing for the boys he'd hit, punched and (probably) kicked. It sounded as if he'd lost or never had the ability to empathise with the plight of others, as if his development had got stuck at the point where a healthy narcissism which builds self-esteem and confidence had become an unhealthy inability to reach beyond himself and connect with the feelings of others. Holmes (2001, p.15) writes: 'Sometimes the narcissist has abandoned hope of mutuality in relationships and relies instead on power and coercion.' There was plenty in the official Liam story to suggest that hitting people might have become his way of having (or of avoiding) relationships with them. I wondered whether there was something about the obvious vulnerability of a boy with a speech difficulty which touched something in Liam which he then had to control ruthlessly. I wondered whether 'dirty looks' were powerful because they threatened to let someone see into him. I wondered how far his behaviour was merely defensive – a response to dangerous situations – and how far it was symptomatic of an inherent inability to feel compassion and to empathise with others.

Work goes on in prisons, trying to discover and train empathy (Robson 2000) in young people whose offences suggest a complete lack of it. For the time being, Liam was still in a mainstream secondary school, still sitting in lessons with everyone else. Although an inability to empathise with others is one indicator of Asperger syndrome, there are other indicators and none of these fitted Liam. Apart from a dangerous inability to empathise which could lead to his exclusion from mainstream schooling altogether and could one day result in his imprisonment, Liam was able to cope. So for now, his new teachers would be trying to help him manage his behaviour while I tried to help him with the feelings (or lack of feelings) provoking such callous attacks. To begin with, my only aim would be to make some kind of relationship with him, however slight and however begrudging that might be.

I found him standing outside my room five minutes after our first session was due to begin. Either it hadn't dawned on him to knock or he'd decided that it wasn't up to him. He responded to me with minimal nods and shakes of the head, making no eye contact. I explained that in our sessions we'd be talking about how things were going in school and we would be talking through those things in detail. With Liam, I planned to keep things business-like to begin with. I remembered how galling it was as a newly-qualified teacher whenever my offer of a friendly relationship was spurned by certain students. All they wanted was a transaction and they much preferred those teachers who offered no more than that. For them, a relationship was too frightening. There was a risk of losing some of their hard-won control, their cool. A relationship may well have been precisely what they most needed – they may have been longing for closeness, for dependence, for things they'd never been able to rely on in their lives – but the risk was too great. The possibility of having those things and losing them again or being exposed by them was too much.

In unfamiliar situations, young people feel safest doing something simple. It was pointless to force the pace and drive Liam into further entrenched cover-ups, so he and I talked in boringly factual detail about his lessons and about the people he was encountering at school. He gave nothing away. He attached no feelings to anything. Still he avoided looking at me.

'Liverpool?' I'd seen the sticker on his school bag.

He nodded.

'We drew with you at Anfield!'

He moved his head. 'You were lucky then!' He didn't bother to ask which rival team I was supporting but glanced at me momentarily and, momentarily, we connected.

Most young people can empathise readily with others. They're therefore able to make close friends and win the approval of adults for being kind and considerate. Schools try to instil as much empathy as possible in the rows of students sitting in assemblies ('Think what it would be like if…!', 'Imagine if you…!') and, quite rightly, local and international charities are supported as opportunities to express that empathy in practical ways. But for a few young people like Liam, empathising is dangerous. It's hard enough feeling their own feelings. Sometimes the energy and physicality (in Liam's case, the brutality) of their behaviour is designed to keep despair and depression at bay, to distract from those lurking sadnesses. Sometimes a stubbornness gets in the way – 'I don't see why I should bother about anyone else, seeing as no one ever bothers about me!' – because, while it's certainly lonely not being able to make friends and not being able to connect with other people's feelings, it can feel safer to cut off from other people altogether and just get through the day without anything happening.

The relationship between Liam and myself needed to be straightforward. It needed to involve me accepting him and all his monosyllabic, shambling hostility. It needed me to be encouraging and prepared to share my own fallibility when that was helpful, rather than set up a one-way relationship in which I kept all the control as chief quizmaster and supreme know-all.

Over the next weeks, we began each session, as planned, by running through the events of the previous week. Liam offered little to begin with, which I took as my punishment for the fact that he hadn't chosen to be there. But some interesting things happened.

Teachers had been picking on him, he insisted. It wasn't fair. Whatever he did, they kept picking on him. I listened to the story, happy that he was ready to be a bit more expansive and interested in what he was saying because I've worked with lots of young people whose first story is always of being picked on. It's the story they tell at the beginning of a session and the story they fall back on whenever the going gets tough and they face having to take responsibility for their behaviour. This story absolves them of that responsibility. Instead, they're endlessly done unto as they sit in a narcissistic cocoon while frustrated teachers, parents and peers try to engage with them. And the more they sit back, the more they really *are* 'picked on' until or unless they find some way of venturing out into a world of mutual respect and shared responsibility. Liam's only way of dealing with this was to come out of the cocoon from time to time and hit people.

He also talked a bit more about his football team: evidence of one attachment to the outside world that he was prepared to acknowledge. I felt pleased. Young people may not always be ready to have a relationship with another human being but they are sometimes able to relate instead to animals, pets, television characters or football teams. When Liverpool lost, Liam admitted to being 'gutted'. When they won, he was 'chuffed'.

We used screwed up balls of paper, in the absence of anything else, to map out Liam's family: big balls for important people, little balls for unimportant people. (We giggled.) He placed them as he saw them in relation to one another – as near or as far as the relationship was close or distant. I asked him what changes he'd like to make and he moved his own ball of paper further from the rest. Oddly, he mentioned his nephew – the smallest bit of paper – to say that his nephew was starting nursery school.

In our next session, I asked again about his nephew. He said Patrick hadn't wanted to go to nursery but apparently had liked it when he got there.

'I spoke to him on the phone. He reckons he's made two friends. I asked him, "Did you beat them up?"'

I smiled, partly at the lengths to which boys must go to disguise affection. I asked if he remembered starting nursery himself.

'I never went.'

'But you know what it's like for Patrick?'

'Because I'm the youngest in my family.'

Liam didn't like being the youngest, he said, and didn't like being treated like a baby, especially by his mother. His eldest brother was a local music DJ. His brother took Liam out in a flashy car and they went to clubs and played pool. His brother had taught him never to let other people mess you about. His brother had been in loads of fights.

I wondered about this relationship. In one sense, Liam was telling me that he was fond of his brother but he was also describing a relationship where he was urged ever onwards by this brother into the anxious, posturing world of young men. Liam's story about his nephew was the parallel story about *not* wanting to make the transition to a more grown-up world. Liam knew what it was like for Patrick, not wanting to go to nursery. I wondered how far he was caught between a wish to *remain* the baby, to retreat from other people's complex demands, and a harsh voice, urging him on, criticising his baby's need to stay safe. Some young people have a particularly harsh version of that voice in their heads, telling them to do this, to do that, to feel this and not that; a voice which, when it becomes intolerable, they sometimes *enact* at other people's expense, punishing others for shortcomings they can no longer bear to recognise in themselves. I wondered whether Liam's violence in school was an imitation of his brother, propping up a bar somewhere, denouncing anything weak or childlike or tender, or whether it was a spontaneous protest against the pressure being put on him by his brother for being weak, childlike, tender. Sanford (1993, p.12) writes of an abused young person: 'When he can no longer stand being a victim, his only choice is to become an offender.'

We'd had five sessions. Miraculously (and because of the skill of his teachers), Liam had done nothing further in those five weeks to risk exclusion from school. He came late for our sixth session because he'd stayed behind to be told off by his History teacher who, predictably, had been picking on him.

I asked him to draw onto a large piece of paper an outline of himself, like the outline of a body drawn at the scene of a murder. I asked him then to tell me all the things other people would say about him who knew him: people at home and at school, his friends and enemies. I wrote the words and phrases down around the outside of the body, prompting him with further questions and suggestions.

We looked at the finished product. He was scornful. 'They don't know nothing!' I explained that this was how other people might see him but that no one knew him as well as he knew himself. We then wrote down *inside* the body the words and phrases Liam felt were true of himself.

Again we looked at the picture, at the differences and the similarities between the inside and the outside. He commented approvingly about two of the phrases inside his body, 'People don't mess me about' and 'I'm not afraid'. Also inside the body, unremarked upon, were 'I get nervous sometimes' and 'I like to have friends'. Suddenly, we were looking at the cocoon from inside and from outside.

Before the session ended, I asked again about his brother and Patrick.

'My brother was in a fight at the weekend.'

I waited for the gory, glorious details.

He looked puzzled. 'My brother told me he was scared.'

This was new.

'How did you feel?'

'I felt a bit sorry for him.'

'A bit sad…?'

'I didn't expect my brother to feel like that.'

Unwittingly, the brother Liam admired (and perhaps resented) for his machismo was modelling something quite different. Liam was absorbing new information.

I left well alone. It's tempting, at moments when something brand new comes to the surface, to seize it triumphantly and shake it about. To develop Liam's capacity to empathise still further, I could have asked him to become his brother in another chair and we could have had an imaginary conversation between the two of them, aiming to deepen Liam's understanding of his brother and, indirectly, give expression to his own 'scared' self. I judged that it was enough for Liam to be thinking about his brother's remark and for us to be thinking about it together.

Our next session was the last of the scheduled, compulsory meetings to which Liam was committed. I was absolutely certain that, although our relationship was much more relaxed, Liam would baulk at the prospect of more sessions, even if they were of his own choosing. I needed to agree an alternative plan with the headteacher.

Liam gave nothing away when I reminded him that this was our last session. I asked how things were.

'My mum's pissing me off!' It was the first time he'd spoken about her, apart from telling me that she treated him as the baby. Again, he described being picked on. He was expected to do things around the house. It wasn't fair. 'I hate her!'

'Because she's hard to talk to?'

'Because I hate her!'

'For what she's done…'

'Yeah.'

'Because she doesn't understand…'

'Yeah.'

'That you're not her little boy any more…'

'That I just want to be left alone.'

'And not criticised…'

'She doesn't get that I can do things on my own, that I don't need her breathing down my neck all the time!'

'That you need her to back off…'

'Yeah.'

'And understand that it's not always as easy as it looks…'

'Exactly! She thinks I should be some kind of boffin!'

We continued in this way, my words echoing and looking to extend the things Liam was able to say about the harsh super-ego he experienced his mother as being. If a young person has never been able to experience pain safely in the presence of an (m)other – someone to listen, to comfort, to amend the hurt – the danger is that the young person learns that it's safer never to experience pain at all – neither his own nor anyone else's. He cuts off. Rather than open Liam up further by myself suggesting feelings he was still unable to name for himself, my concern was to consolidate what he *had* been able to say and to keep those things safe within our relationship: listening, comforting and, by virtue of sharing them together, beginning to amend the hurt.

It's sometimes suggested (Kernberg 1992) that pathological aggression (the kind Liam had exhibited in school) is effectively a protest against unresponsive mothering. If a person has too little experience of holding on safely to a mother figure, loving and being loved, he or she may hold on instead to a hatred of her. In other words, Liam's violence may have been an expression of the hatred he *could* feel towards a mother for whom he couldn't feel love, probably because she had no idea how to love him. Liam had never told me about traumatic events in his life (I had no idea what had happened to his father, for example) but there are plenty of young people who do carry such events around as hardening lumps of quite brutally denied feeling.

I described to Liam the plan I'd hatched with the headteacher's approval. He and I would continue to meet for as long as we chose but each week we would be able to go out of school. This wouldn't be 'counselling' as such. It would be fun and different. We could go to cafes or record shops or to the market or wherever we fancied during the brief time we had each week.

'What if I don't want to go?'

I explained that this would be okay. Instead of coming out of school with me, he would stay in his normal lesson.

So we spent several more weeks walking out of school together, drinking coffee, joking about my hapless football team and talking. My thinking was simply that, the longer our relationship lasted, the more Liam would absorb of warmth and humour between two human beings and the less cut off he would remain from the feelings inside himself.

In response to another conversation about being 'pissed off', I made him a compilation tape of angry songs by different bands in different styles. I wanted to alert him to the fact that his anger was echoed by other people. My hope was that there would be songs on the tape which touched, expressed and extended feelings already in Liam.

He made me a tape of his favourite rap music, all of it by men, all of it full of anger, full of people being pissed off and things being unfair.

I made him another tape of songs expressing a wider range of feelings by men and by women: songs of sadness, pity, love and longing as well as anger. He said he liked 'some of it'. In return, I received a tape of more rap music, still pissed off, still unfair, but with two songs by women and with some less frenetic moments.

It would be naive to imagine that lasting change in a young person exhibiting psychopathic (unempathic) behaviour like Liam can be achieved through one person, a weekly meeting and a friendly relationship. I've described ways in which that relationship and those weekly meetings might be a means of developing a young person's ability (and willingness) to empathise with others. I haven't described the daily work of other professionals, especially teachers, which must also (and does) go on in containing the young person safely, in praising good behaviour and in explaining why other behaviour is inappropriate or hurtful to others. Both kinds of work are necessary and complement each other. Nor have I yet described what might be the next phase of a young person's rehabilitation into the world of feelings and the next phase of my work with Liam: the experience of being in a group.

Young people have mixed feelings about groups. On the one hand, groups mean friends and fun. It's a relief for most young people to find out through being in a group that they're actually *like* other young people because their fear is that they're bound to discover the opposite. But groups also potentially mean enemies and persecution. I imagined Liam wouldn't be afraid of enemies because he'd inured himself to that. I imagined his fear would actually be of finding out that he was *like* other boys and then not knowing what to do.

We sat in a circle. Each chair had a number. Number one had to say his number, followed by another person's number. That person then had to say his own number, followed by someone else's, but he wasn't allowed to say the number of the person who just said his and he couldn't stumble, hesitate or get the numbers muddled up in any way. If he made any of these mistakes, he had to go and sit in the bottom chair (number 12, because there were 12 of us in the group) and everyone would move round one chair to fill the space he'd left. So if number four made a mistake, he went to chair 12, the person in chair five moved into chair four, the person in chair six into chair five and so on; chairs one, two and three remained unaffected. Everyone's aim was to get to sit in chair number one.

We played the game, continuing around the circle. Mistakes were made. People moved chairs, got muddled and moved again, trying to remember to answer on behalf of the chair on which they were now sitting.

Once they'd got the hang of it, I changed the rules. This time I gave each chair a different piece of card with the name of a feeling on it. 'Lonely' began and off we went, 'Lonely, Happy!', 'Happy, Angry!', 'Angry, Sad!', 'Sad, Frustrated!'. As mistakes were made and he changed chairs, Liam answered on behalf of several different feelings.

The group had come about because I'd been talking with his form tutor. We'd decided that for six weeks I would work with the boys during their lesson while she worked with the girls. In a café nearby, Liam and I had talked about what this would be like for both of us. He'd said he didn't like the boys in his tutor group, which I took to mean that he thought they didn't like him and, above all, that he didn't think he was *like* them. He'd avoided mentioning Ricky, the boy with the speech difficulty.

I changed the rules again. Now, instead of numbers, each chair was named after the person currently sitting in it. We began again. Someone stumbled and half the group moved chairs. Liam moved along from the 'Liam' chair to sit in the 'Jonathan' chair. Now he had to answer to 'Jonathan' while someone else answered as 'Liam'. Another boy made a mistake. We moved chairs again and Liam became 'Mohammed'. The top chair called, 'Steve, Mohammed!'

'Mohammed, Chris!' He was on his way, answering to someone else's name...

We did an exercise where one person sat with his back to the group. Silently, the rest of us chose another person in the group to describe and we took turns to describe that person *positively*. The boy with his back to the group had to guess who was being described. When he'd succeeded, someone else had a turn to be the guesser with someone else being described and off we went again. And again. We then did another exercise where one boy went out and, in his absence, people said positive things about him. He came back in and heard what had been said. His task was to identify who'd said each of the things about him. Again, we took turns to be the person going out of the room.

For a group of boys to say positive things about one another is hard. It provokes all manner of homophobic anxiety. Over the weeks that followed, we did plenty of exercises to make these anxieties more bearable. Tentatively, we did some trust exercises. We also discussed hypothetical problems *other* young people might be experiencing: problems with friendships, bullying, families and so on. We did 'Boss and Slave' where for two minutes one partner can command the other to do whatever he says (within reason) before the roles are reversed and the slave becomes the boss for two minutes.

Liam coped with these exercises and in our weekly meetings away from school we discussed how he was finding the group. Where, once upon a time, they were 'a bunch of complete tossers', he was now less inclined to pass judgement on the other boys. We'd done an exercise, spread over several weeks, where each boy took a turn to become and answer questions as if he were another boy in the group, *imagining* whatever he didn't already know for sure about the other boy in order to answer the questions. By asking questions which had to have more than a one-word answer, the group had to guess who this boy was pretending to be. So far, no one had pretended to be Liam and Liam hadn't had his turn to be someone else. I reminded him of this.

'Hope I don't have to do it!'

'Because it's hard to know what it's like being someone else?'

'Because I don't want to *be* anyone else!'

'Because it might be hard to know how they'd feel?'

'Yeah!'

'They probably feel much like you.'

'I doubt it!'

'They probably feel angry a lot of the time and sad sometimes but they try to cover that up. And they probably wish they were stronger and cleverer and more popular...'

'Yeah, all right,' he interrupted. 'Don't go on!'

We laughed.

'Imagine if you had to be Ricky,' I said.

'I'd refuse!'

'No you wouldn't. You could imagine what it would be like, not being properly understood because of your voice, being teased, wanting to have friends but finding that hard...'

Liam said nothing. I gave him the money and he paid for our coffees.

At the next group session, a boy called Daniel chose to be Ricky. When it was his turn to ask a question, Liam said, 'How do you get on with *me*?'

'I'm scared of you,' Daniel said as Ricky. 'I never know what you're thinking. You don't like me.'

Once we'd guessed whom he was pretending to be, I asked Ricky to correct anything Daniel had said in his name. (There's an important difference between someone merely projecting his own feelings onto someone else and a person actually empathising with another person.) Ricky said Daniel had got it mostly right except that his speech difficulty didn't make him angry because he was used to it.

I reminded Liam of what Daniel (as Ricky) had said about him. I asked him whether Daniel had got that right.

Liam glared at me. 'No!'

I asked what he'd got wrong.

'He said I don't like him. That's not true! I think he's okay, in some ways.'

We had time for one more turn. Liam volunteered, 'to get it over with'. He pretended to be Jonathan and did a reasonable job, answering a glum 'don't know' to the questions which required most imagination (most empathy) but managing to answer other questions about school, exams, favourite holidays and wanting a job in the police: answers which Jonathan later confirmed were accurate.

It was the sixth and final week of the group. Only Ricky was still to have a turn and only Liam hadn't been impersonated. We acknowledged that Ricky nevertheless had a choice: he could pretend to be Liam or he could double-bluff and pretend to be someone else who'd already been impersonated.

Steve asked, 'How do you get on with your mum?'

Ricky answered, 'We don't get on that well.'

Mohammed asked, 'How do you like being in this tutor group?'

Ricky answered, 'I used to hate it. Everyone had their own little friendship groups. I think it's all right now.'

Usman asked him, 'Do you fancy the girls?'

Ricky said, 'Of course I do!'

Chris asked, 'Do they fancy you?'

'Not as much as they should!'

Everyone laughed.

Liam asked a question which had become standard in the group: 'What's your biggest fear?'

Ricky answered straightaway, 'Being hated. I act like I don't care but I do really.'

There was silence while they tried to work out which of them this might be.

Andy asked, 'What makes you angry?'

Ricky said, 'People who don't like me.'

I asked, 'What makes you laugh?'

Ricky answered, 'Man United losing!'

Heads immediately turned to Liam. He grinned. A few more boys asked their questions but they'd already guessed because they all knew perfectly well that Liam supported Liverpool. Ricky had given it away. I asked Liam to say something about the other things Ricky had said. He confirmed that 'some of them were right'.

'So you do fancy the girls!' said Usman.

'Maybe…!' Liam twisted in his chair but he was grinning. He was part of the group. They were joking with him and he was responding.

Two years later, I saw him walking out of school for the last time – flour in his hair and his white shirt covered in felt-pen graffiti – just like the others, also leaving school, walking beside him.

The anger of professionals (again)

Why is it that whenever I run training workshops for teachers, exploring their relationships with those students whom they find most difficult, so many teachers are suddenly so keen to volunteer for the role of the angry or disaffected student? Often our workshop is remembered, not for the careful insights or strategies we discovered, but for how realistically that particular role was played by the teacher, how much the teacher swore and grumbled, how clearly we recognised the portrayal of the student and how much we all laughed.

I remember a teacher who seemed very prim and proper, very *reserved*, describing a boy with whom she couldn't get on. He wouldn't wear his school uniform, wouldn't be polite to her, wouldn't do any work.

We moved the furniture and set up an imaginary scene in her classroom. I invited her to become this student so that we might better understand him.

Immediately she came to life, muttering sarcastically, slouching in the chair, sullen and stubborn and rude. Something came alive for her in playing the role of the disaffected boy which previously she'd kept hidden beneath a heavy professional calm.

Such calm is, of course, absolutely necessary in order to model sensible behaviour and reassure students that, while all around may be losing their heads, the teachers, at least, are in control. But I think that for many teachers and other professionals working with young people, the pressure of keeping their own disaffected voice quiet becomes intolerable.

Earlier in the workshop people had talked about the kind of teacher they'd become (or wanted to become) in relation to the kind of parenting they'd experienced in their own lives. They were interested in the connection. This teacher described herself as being like her mother who was always the boss, she said; a much more powerful figure at home than her father. Her mother was someone whose expectations were high and were clearly to be lived up to.

We listened. I think this teacher had got stuck in her relationship with the boy partly because her relationship with *that part of herself* had got stuck. A disaffected part clearly existed somewhere inside her or she wouldn't have been able to take on and play that role so vividly. Why, then, had she got stuck?

However old we may be, our parents still have an effect on us and, in many cases, that effect is carried into our daily adult lives. It may well have been that the disaffected boy reminded this teacher of parts of herself she'd never been able to express in her life, parts of herself never expressed at home which she therefore still carried around inside her as unexploded bombs.

I've worked with many teachers who have been full of anger for the things life has thrown at them. For them, containing that anger has been debilitating. One person, the youngest boy in a family where the older children were favoured, fought constantly with authority figures throughout his teenage years, underachieving academically and getting expelled from two schools. His unconscious logic in becoming a teacher (a particularly severe teacher) seemed to be that he would deal with his anger by becoming his own authority figure. By controlling the anger of so many students he would succeed in controlling his own. But his anger wouldn't be controlled so easily and teaching was therefore proving to be a difficult job.

Another teacher seemed to be offering her students all the things she herself had never experienced. From an early age she'd become the family carer, nursing her mother and siblings once her father had run off. Now she was continuing in the role, working ceaselessly and expertly to provide students with care and a sense of personal worth. Yet she'd come to see me because she felt like giving up teaching. It seemed that, the more she gave, the more empty she felt inside. If her original logic had been that she would find nourishment in nourishing others, it hadn't worked.

There's nothing unusual about adults still searching for what they needed as children. What makes it complicated is when those adults are working with children whose needs are actually similar to their own and, because they *are* children, so much more overt. Then things can get muddled.

Whether they like it or not, teachers work in loco parentis. They get called Mum. They are parent figures in the classroom, taking charge, knowing best, sorting out endless squabbles. Most teachers recognise that, to do the job adequately, this parental ('pastoral') role is inescapable and most take it on generously and conscientiously. Yet teachers can't help but remind students of *real* parents and therefore they attract positive and negative responses from students which often have little to do with themselves as teachers and everything to do with the students' feelings about *actual* parents, the ones at home. Feelings about these parents are brought in on the bus in the morning and expressed at unsuspecting teachers' expense during the rest of the day.

Those parents at home, meanwhile, tidying up before going off to work, are full of feelings themselves, sometimes idealising and sometimes demonising the teachers, grateful to them or hugely resentful. It's hard for parents to have an objective view of the adult who spends so much time with their child. A standard piece of work, set by teachers for perfectly understandable reasons at the beginning of a year with a new class, is for students each to write something called 'Myself'. Parents read this carefully. What sort of impression has my child created? How have I been portrayed as a parent? What assumptions will the new teacher make, reading this partial account of an 11-year-old life? As a teacher, I remember marking these pieces with a kind of glee. It may be that teachers unconsciously set this first piece of work as a way of establishing their position as 'new' parents and as a way of worrying the 'old' parents. 'Myself' can't be faulted as a sensible, straightforward first piece of work and yet it can be *so* personal, *so* revealing…

'Myself' may be only one of many roundabout ways in which teachers fight back. They, too, can demonise. They, too, can be resentful. When they complain that they just want to get on with teaching and not – as they put it – 'become social workers', I think they really complain about the demands of working as parent figures. In almost every training workshop I run, the issue is raised which besets teachers just as it does parents: how strict or how lenient should I be? One student will be sitting there at the back of the classroom, complaining that the teacher is being too strict, while another sits at the front, complaining that the teacher is being far too lenient. Most teachers probably do err on one side or the other and that's to do with confidence and experience. But it's also to do with the impossibility of getting it right for all the students all the time. Children and young people want it both ways. When a teacher *can* strike enough of a balance and students *can* learn to live with both structure and freedom in the classroom, it serves as a vitally corrective experience for those students who have only ever experienced one or the other at home. For some students, rules at home are enforced ruthlessly or not at all.

Faced with this, teachers have to live with a perpetual sense of inadequacy. They know that, however thorough their preparation, however committed they may be, their best lesson will still probably only fully engage three quarters of the class. Living with this is hard. So teachers redouble their efforts with relentless *doing*. To pause and to reflect seems like time-wasting and, in any case, to reflect is to be reminded. So they don't. Instead they beg their managers for clarity, for simplicity: 'Just tell me what to do and I'll do it!' But their sense of inadequacy is really the inadequacy of parents, knowing they are responsible for but can never wholly control their child's development. The task is too complex. Teachers' despair is then sometimes directed at students in the same way as parents blaming their child: 'I despair of you!'

I worked in a school where a special unit was set up for the most disaffected students and three members of staff were given the job of running it. They began work but within a matter of weeks things had begun to fall apart. One member of staff had somehow become the enforcer, barking at everyone and constantly having rows with students about discipline. The second member of staff had become a laid-back, nurturing pillow for students to cuddle. And the third member of staff, caught in the middle, wanted to resign.

No doubt each of them had their own reasons for choosing to work with disaffected students in the first place and no doubt the roles they found themselves playing came partly from their individual family histories. But I think that the unit found itself expressing something on behalf of the school about whether the school's real task was to process students through as many exams as quickly as possible or whether its task was to love students so that they became happier. The conflict was unspoken and unresolved in the school and was dramatised (Hinshelwood 2001) spectacularly by the unit. Any middle ground – a combination of authority and kindness – was uncomfortable and so, not surprisingly, the third member of staff, attempting to steer a course through such polarised waters, felt like giving up.

Such a conflict will always be near the surface of a unit like this anyway, simply because young people carry it around with them all the time: needing parent figures to be both authoritative *and* kind, but claiming always to need one and not the other. And the most disaffected young people, in my experience, are usually the most skilled at getting staff to enact the conflict (Obholzer and Roberts 1994).

Teachers are also, effectively, *single* parents. They may spend time with other 'single parents' in the staffroom, but when the bell rings they return alone to their classroom to manage their own children. One of the most dangerous things a teacher can do is to criticise another's students. Then the 'parental' hackles rise because, not only are the students being criticised (*my* students), but, by implication, so is their teacher: 'That doesn't sound like my class! They're not usually like that!'

Headteachers are also set up to be single parents, fiercely protective towards their teachers but also exasperated by them. Interestingly, another important figure usually emerges in a school, by no means always the deputy headteacher, who becomes a second parent figure, thereby creating a version of the parental couple. As in families, they often complement each other in style, in tone, in approach and, although the second figure is less powerful in the hierarchy, he or she becomes no less important within the school. I can think of many schools where this phenomenon occurs, as if the unconscious mind of the school requires it and so, as if by magic, it happens: the autocratic headteacher balanced by the kindly deputy; the rational balanced by the emotional, the chaotic balanced by the orderly. Indeed, thoughtful headteachers – knowing this – will appoint deputies *not* in their own image but deputies whose strengths will complement their own.

The more teachers have this role of responsible, all-encompassing parent thrust upon them, the more powerful becomes the opposite, angry urge to misbehave, to subvert, to regress. In popular staffroom mythology, for example, the local education authority is always made up of incompetent dimwits who have no understanding of classroom reality. When one of these dimwits comes to address a staff meeting, the rush to fill up the giggling back row is more frantic than ever. The staffroom defends against its own (perfectly understandable) sense of inadequacy by ascribing any inadequacy to the hopeless dimwits in the smart suits.

Whether because of the intrinsically parental nature of the role or because of personal history, many teachers identify with and therefore struggle more with disaffected students than they might otherwise do. They, too, want to swear, to be difficult, to refuse to do as they're told and they, too, (secretly) want to be looked after.

Excluding impossible students from school is always agonising (like telling your child to go and find somewhere else to live) and some students *do* behave terribly. But excluding them may also be accompanied by the belief that everything will feel better from now on: teachers' own feelings of inadequacy and disaffection will go away along with the excluded student who has come to embody them so vividly. Sadly, it doesn't take long before another student emerges as the official staffroom bogey-student.

Perhaps (as I suggested in Chapter 2) at some unconscious level, we all choose the particular jobs we do, not only to earn money or prestige, but to resolve internal conflicts of our own. That may be what 'job satisfaction' really means. Lawyers may resolve something important inside themselves, for example, when the mental processes and clarity of the law succeed yet again in overcoming the physical chaos of living. Others may aim to resolve deeply rooted feelings about parenting or about authority by becoming teachers.

If there's truth in this and there's rather more to our relationships at work than we commonly suppose, how do we prevent ourselves from becoming stuck? If, for all sorts of reasons, we actually identify with disruptive students, we need time to think about and so take control of that identification or else we risk being dragged into prolonged and messy wars. Students will, without fail, affect us. If there are no ways of dealing with this, no opportunities to think about what's happening, 'stress' may become our only way of expressing dissent, of saying no. Sometimes teachers also refuse to go to school.

One teacher I know, who has stayed open to learning and compassionate towards students after many years at the sharp end of teaching, showed me the Lake District photo he keeps on his classroom desk. He 'goes there' in his head when he needs to. I think what he means is that he's found a way, not of escaping, but of separating himself from his professional role sometimes in order not to get caught up in the maelstrom of feelings in which he, as a teacher, is bound to operate. I suspect this accounts for the fact that he's still teaching enthusiastically after a very long time.

Another teacher told me about leaving school at the end of the day, raging at the way she felt treated by students, by other staff and by the world. She was still raging when she arrived (late!) for her evening painting class. Ignoring the task set, she painted a single scarlet flower, a chrysanthemum, doing it quickly and carelessly. Yet it emerged as the most satisfying painting she'd ever done, bold and bright and alive. Somehow her rage – and the opportunity to paint it – had tapped into something she felt unable to express at school where she was bogged down in a responsible role.

One of the reasons why so many teachers choose to get involved in extra-curricular activities with students is because, in doing these activities, they can be different. They can step out of their more formal parental role and enjoy a different kind of relationship. When they return from school trips, they inevitably enthuse about having been able to be more 'relaxed' with the students.

Without opportunities to step out of role and reflect on what exactly it is that we're doing in working with young people, the danger is that our identifications, our histories, our frustrations and abiding sense of inadequacy all become too much. We explode. Our relationships at home suffer. We blame other people. We stagnate. We become ill.

I've worked with a faith school where saying prayers at the start of staff meetings seemed to have the effect of calming teachers, allowing them to step back from their immediate concerns and put themselves into perspective. In another school, I remember a teacher beginning the lesson with a potentially difficult class of 15-year-olds by playing calm, tape-recorded music as they entered. As she'd taught them to do, they sat comfortably and closed their eyes while she talked them gently through the trials and tribulations of their day so far. She invited them to leave any feelings of frustration and disappointment behind and begin to focus on the lesson to come. To my surprise, the class seemed to relish this opportunity to reflect for a few minutes before getting down to their normal work which they did with purpose. I imagine that many of their teachers would have valued the same opportunity.

Some teachers I know have set up formal opportunities to reflect regularly on the relationship between themselves and their work with a consultant employed from outside the school. They tease out identifications, untangle blocks and, in so doing, are able to feel more focused, more creative, more relaxed. In some professions, it would be inconceivable, if not unethical, to do a job, the success of which depends so much on the quality of the relationships, without a regular opportunity to think through those relationships. I think this is not only a good use of professional time, but ultimately about job satisfaction and effectiveness.

Towards the end of term, a teacher asks to see me. She sits down to talk, her eyes filling immediately with tears. 'Can I swear?' she asks, very politely.

References

Adshead, G. (2001) *Three Degrees of Security: Attachment and Interpersonal Violence.* Unpublished talk given to the Oxford Psychotherapy Society.

Ainsworth, M., Blehar, M., Waters, E. and Wall, S. (1978) *Patterns of Attachment.* Hillsdale, NJ: Erlbaum.

Balindt, M. (1968) *The Basic Fault.* London: Hogarth Press.

Bannister, A. (2002) 'The effects of creative therapies with children who have been sexually abused.' *The British Journal of Psychodrama and Sociodrama 17,* 2, 3–18.

Bowlby, J. (1969) *Attachment and Loss. Vol. 1, Attachment.* London: Hogarth Press.

Bowlby, J. (1973) *Attachment and Loss. Vol. 2, Separation: Anxiety and Anger.* London: Hogarth Press.

Bowlby, J. (1980) *Attachment and Loss. Vol. 3, Sadness and Depression.* London: Hogarth Press.

Bronowski, J. (ed.) (1958) *A Selection of Poems and Letters.* London: Penguin.

Coren, A. (1997) *A Psychodynamic Approach to Education.* London: Sheldon Press.

Dahl, R. (1988) *Matilda.* London: Jonathan Cape.

Davies, R. (1997) 'A violent child and his family.' In Ved Varma (ed.) *Violence in Children and Adolescents.* London: Jessica Kingsley Publishers.

Faupel, A., Herrick, E. and Sharp, P. (1998) *Anger Management.* London: David Fulton Publishers.

Fonagy, P. (2004) 'The developmental roots of violence in the failure of mentalisation.' In F. Pfafflin and G. Adshead (eds) *A Matter of Security: The Application of Attachment Theory to Forensic Psychiatry and Psychotherapy.* London: Jessica Kingsley Publishers.

Freud, S. (1911) *Formulations on the Two Principles of Mental Functioning.* Standard Edition 12. London: Hogarth Press.

Freud, S. (1920) *Beyond the Pleasure Principle.* Standard Edition 18. London: Hogarth Press.

Freud, S. (1927) *The Future of an Illusion.* Standard Edition 21. London: Hogarth Press.

Gerhardt, S. (2004) *Why Love Matters: How Affection Shapes a Baby's Brain.* Hove: Brunner-Routledge.

Hinshelwood, R.D. (2001) *Thinking about Institutions.* London: Jessica Kingsley Publishers.

Hodgson Burnett, F. (1911) *The Secret Garden.* London: (Puffin) Penguin Books.

Holmes, J. (2001) *Narcissism.* Cambridge: Icon Books.

Jacobs, M. (1998) *The Presenting Past.* Buckingham: Open University Press.

Jones, T. (1981) *Fairy Tales.* London: Pavilion Books.

Kernberg, O.T. (1992) *Aggression in Personality Disorders and Perversions.* London and New Haven: Yale University Press.

Klein, J. (1987) *Our Need for Others and its Roots in Infancy.* London: Tavistock Publications.

Klein, M. (1935) 'A contribution to the psychogenesis of manic-depressive states.' *The International Journal of Psycho-Analysis 16*, 145–174.

Klein, M. (1957) *Envy and Gratitude: A Study of Unconscious Sources.* London: Tavistock Publications.

Kohut, H. (1971) *The Analysis of the Self.* New York: International University Press.

Lacan, J. (1949) 'Le stade du miroir.' In *Ecrits* (1966). Paris: Editions du Seuil.

Lomas, P. (1987) *The Limits of Interpretation.* London: Constable Publishers.

Luxmoore, N. (2000) *Listening to Young People in School, Youth Work and Counselling.* London: Jessica Kingsley Publishers.

Marvel Comics (2000) *The Incredible Hulk – Psyche-out!* 1, 19. New York: Marvel Comics.

Meltzer, D. and Williams, M.H. (1988) *The Apprehension of Beauty.* Strath Tay: The Clunie Press.

Mitchell, J. (ed.) (1991) *The Selected Melanie Klein.* London: Penguin.

Mollon, P. (2002) *Shame and Jealousy: The Hidden Turmoils.* London: Karnac Books.

Obholzer, A. and Roberts, V.Z. (1994) *The Unconscious at Work.* London: Routledge.

Panksepp, J., Siviy, S.M. and Normansell, L.A. (1985) 'Brain opioids and social emotions.' In M. Reite and T. Field (eds) *The Psychobiology of Attachment and Separation.* Orlando, FL: Academic Press.

Pfäfflin, F. and Adshead, G. (2003) *A Matter of Security: The Application of Attachment Theory to Forensic Psychiatry and Psychotherapy.* London: Jessica Kingsley Publishers.

Phillips, A. (1994) *On Flirtation.* London: Faber.

Pincus, L. (1976) *Death and the Family.* London: Faber.

Robson, M. (2000) 'Psychodrama with adolescent sexual offenders.' In P.F. Kellerman and M.K. Hudgins (eds) *Psychodrama with Trauma Survivors.* London: Jessica Kingsley Publishers.

Rose, J. (2001) 'Absence and inertia in the transference: some problems encountered when treating young men who have become developmentally stuck.' In G. Baruch (ed.) *Community-based Psychotherapy with Young People.* Hove: Brunner-Routledge.

Rothschild, B. (2000) *The Body Remembers: The Psychophysiology of Trauma and Trauma Treatment.* New York: W.W. Norton.

Rothschild, B. (2004) 'The physiology of empathy.' *Counselling and Psychotherapy Journal 15*, 9, 11–15. Rugby: The British Association for Counselling and Psychotherapy.

Salzberger-Wittenberg, I. (1970) *Psycho-Analytic Insight and Relationships.* London: Routledge.

Sanford, L.T. (1993) *Strong at the Broken Places: Overcoming the Trauma of Child Abuse.* London: Virago.

Schore, A.N. (1994) *Affect Regulation and the Origin of the Self.* Hillsdale, NJ, and Hove: Lawrence Erlbaum.

Storr, A. (1972) *The Dynamics of Creation.* London: Secker & Warburg.

Storr, A. (1996) *Feet of Clay.* London: HarperCollins Publishers.

Suttie, I.D. (1935) *The Origins of Love and Hate.* London: Kegan Paul.

Van Sant, G. (1997) *Good Will Hunting.* New York: Miramax.

Winnicott, D.W. (1965a) *The Family and Individual Development.* London: Tavistock Publications.

Winnicott, D.W. (1965b) *The Maturational Processes and the Facilitating Environment.* London: Hogarth Press.

Winnicott, D.W. (1971) *Playing and Reality.* London: Routledge.

Winnicott, D.W. (1975) *Through Paediatrics to Psychoanalysis.* London: Tavistock Publications.

Winnicott, D.W. (1986) *Home is Where we Start From.* London: Penguin Books.

Yalom, I.D. (2001) *The Gift of Therapy.* New York: HarperCollins Publishers.

Subject index

Author index